ISLANDS OF THE SOUTH

Islands
of the South

Austin Coates

HEINEMANN · LONDON

Heinemann Educational Books Ltd
LONDON EDINBURGH MELBOURNE AUCKLAND TORONTO
HONG KONG SINGAPORE KUALA LUMPUR
IBADAN NAIROBI JOHANNESBURG
NEW DELHI

ISBN 0 435 32208 7

Published by Heinemann Educational Books Ltd
48 Charles Street, London W1X 8AH
Printed in Great Britain by
William Clowes & Sons, Limited
London, Beccles and Colchester

To

ANTONIO B. BANTUG

and

ASUNCIÓN LÓPEZ RIZAL BANTUG

my two dearest friends in the Islands of the South

Acknowledgements

I wish to record my thanks for the help I have received from two personal friends: the eminent South-East Asian architect Lim Chong Keat, for his criticisms, advice on references, and help with the illustrations; and fellow-writer Sjovald Cunyngham-Brown, formerly of the Malayan Civil Service, for his advice on numerous points concerned with Pacific and Oriental linguistics and navigation.

Contents

Illustrations

Pour comprendre son présent, pour essayer de percer les ténèbres de son avenir, l'homme a besoin de reconstituer aussi complètement que possible son passé.

JACQUES SOUSTELLE : *Les quatre soleils*

Introduction

In the study of the world as we know it not stands the prehistoric Austronesian civilization.

Of Pacific origin, it seems to have been at its zenith around 3500 B.C., prior to the First Dynasty of Egypt. It relates to a time when men and women were sailing in conditions of relative peace throughout an area which extended from Tahiti to Madagascar. It is a civilization which left no monuments, and had no handwriting.

The suggestion that men and women were peacefully sailing halfway round the world thousands of years ago immediately plunges the subject into a realm of fantasy, so improbable does it seem. The spread of the Austronesian languages, all derived from a single parent language, and their age, must serve to dispel any idea that this is fantasy. Approximately 180,000,000 people, living between Madagascar and the Eastern Pacific, are this very day speaking to each other in their homes in Austronesian languages, or else lying asleep dreaming Austronesian dreams.

It has for long been generally considered that the islands of the Pacific are in some unknown way cultural and genetic offshoots of Asia. Yet nothing has ever come to light in the Pacific to give substance to this view. Each time a Pacific scholar endeavours to establish a relationship of derivation from Asia to the Pacific, his theory breaks down at the first approach of Oriental study. Even in Melanesia, which abuts Asia, there is no trace whatever of Asiatic influence or origin. Such prehistoric influences as penetrated Melanesia are exclusively Oceanic.

To a long-time observer of this general region, familiar with its people, their character and culture, what is salient in the evident relationship between Asia and the Pacific is, directionally speaking, the opposite to that commonly held, namely, Oceania's influence on the Orient.

The people of South-East Asia have an important strain of Pacific ancestry. Many of them, notably in Indonesia and the Philippines, are culturally Pacific people, whose connexions with the Oriental world began at a comparatively recent date – little more than three thousand years ago. The Pacific, in fact, supplied one of the major elements which have made Asia what it is today.

At some unknown date, not later than 3500 B.C., large numbers of people from the Pacific, skilled in navigation and astronomy, came westward into Asia, driven by population pressure, at a time when China and India were inland civilizations, having nowhere a coastline.[1]

Their subsequent fortunes in Asia, their widespread influence, discernible today in the lives of many in South-East Asia, and the consequences of their arrival, are the theme of this study.

Since for the inquirer of today they left only their languages and themselves, in the shape of descendants, any examination of them begins essentially in the present. Many people who today speak Austronesian languages are not of Oceanic origin. These include the principal tribal people of South-East Asia, and nearly all Melanesians. The question is: how is a person of Oceanic origin identified?

Part I of what follows deals with this question, indicating certain human characteristics displayed in Asia which have their origins in Oceania.

In Part II the setting is shifted to a Pacific atoll, where these same human characteristics are observed in their original social framework, the source whence they derive. In addition, various other features of atoll life are discussed in relation to Asia.

Part III deals with matters of adaptation. The transposition from the continent of water, which is what Oceania is, to Asia, a continent of land, presents human society with one of the most demanding challenges the world can offer, the two forms of life – Oceanic and continental – being so different they might almost belong to

[1] Appendices will be found at the end of this volume, explaining how some of the principal dates are arrived at. The appendices will be footnoted at appropriate points in the text.

separate planets. First, Pacific people will be observed in relation to Asia and the people already living there, who did not have the same problems as they. Next, their adaptation – or lack of it – to commerce will be examined. This is such an extraordinary story it really deserves a book to itself. Finally, Oceanic government will be explained, and briefly traced to its extinction in Asia.

Each of these first three parts is a prelude, the three combined being designed to give the reader sufficient general understanding of the subject to be able to read the fourth and principal part, which is an attempted reconstruction of the past. Beginning from the most remote times in Oceania, and treating prehistory as if it were history, this traces the Austronesian people into Asia, following their fortunes down to the coming of Europeans and history.

There is a particular reason for bringing the recital down so close as this to the present. The megalithic and Hindu periods in South-East Asia, lying in the field of Oriental studies, have hitherto been approached by scholars with an Asiatic standpoint. As a result, they are not at present attached to the body to which they properly belong, which is an Oceanic body.

By relating the two, as is done here, various puzzling features of Overseas Hinduism explain themselves, enabling this interesting and unusual period to be seen more clearly.

With this, the descendants of the Austronesian civilization advance with a degree less mystery from the shadows of their immense past into the light of day.

PART I

Austronesia in the Contemporary World

Kitam menurok-kan anak-nya berjalan betul.[1]
Indonesian Proverb

---

[1] Crabs teaching their young to walk head forwards.

I The Austronesian Region in Asia

What does the map of the Orient show in terms of men and money ?
It sounds a strange question. A map tells little enough of men,
still less about money. Yet draw an imaginary line across it, separating parts of the south from the north, and it reflects an inner truth
about the Orient concerned with men and money.

The line can begin on the western side of the Orient, somewhere in
the Arabian Sea. Projecting eastwards, it passes south of Cape
Comorin, the southernmost point of India, thence north-eastwards
between India and Ceylon, having the effect of separating Ceylon
from continental Asia.

Thence it proceeds eastward across the Bay of Bengal, passing
just to the north of the island of Sumatra, and crossing the Malay
peninsula in the region of the southernmost provinces of Thailand.
This will have the effect of separating Malaya from continental Asia.

At this point the line enters the South China Sea, and remains in
it. After skirting the coast of Vietnam, it heads north-east, passing
between the Philippines and China. Immediately north of the
Philippines it swings sharply east, then northward again, passing to
the east of Taiwan and Japan, and ending up anywhere in the North
Pacific Ocean.

North and west of this line, in the continental Orient, men
understand how to handle and utilize money, or in the case of a
country such as Thailand, a sufficiently large number of people
understand money and its utilization to cause money to circulate in a
healthy fashion and an economy to exist. South and east of the line,
in Insular Asia, the number of indigenous people who understand
money and its utilization is so small that money does not circulate
in a healthy fashion among them, and there is no economy in the
proper sense of that word. In the place of economy stands exploitation, benefiting an exceptionally small percentage of the population,

leaving great numbers who are only just living on a money economy.

This southerly region, as delineated, is the part of Asia which exhibits the strongest surviving traces of the prehistoric Austronesian civilization, and will be the focal point of observation. Excluding Ceylon, all the principal languages spoken are of Austronesian derivation.

The region being insular save for the Malay peninsula, it will be referred to here as Insular Asia.

Geographically, it consists of Ceylon, the Indonesian archipelago, the Malay peninsula, Borneo, Celebes, the Moluccas, and the Philippines.[1] The Indonesian archipelago is sometimes taken to include Borneo, Celebes and the Moluccas. Here, for the sake of clarity, these islands will be treated as separate geographical units, the Indonesian archipelago being taken to refer solely to the long chain of volcanic islands stretching from Sumatra to Timor.

In general, traditional English spellings of place-names will be used. Celebes is described in Indonesia today as Sulawesi, which is an indonesianization of the more widely known former name Celebes, which is itself a corruption of the original Portuguese name, Ponta dos Celebres. The Moluccas are known in Indonesia as Maluku, a version of the name Maluco, by which these islands first became known to the Portuguese and Spaniards. Ceylon has recently changed its name to Sri Lanka, which is an Indian name for that island. Here the earlier name Ceylon will be used, as given to the Portuguese – Ceilão – meaning the home of the Singhala people.

Though the Austronesian-derived tongues are currently referred to as the Malayo-Polynesian group of languages, this term will not be used. Being partly ethnic and partly geographic, it is confusing; and while linguistically it applies well enough to present conditions, it does not apply to the prehistoric past. For this reason the older and purely geographical word is used – Austronesia, the Islands of the South.

There are a number of other confusing terms used in the region. The Indonesians are sometimes referred to as a Malayan people,

[1] The 'Malay' peninsula is British usage. The more widely used geographical name is Malacca peninsula.

while Filipinos frequently refer to themselves as members of the Malay or Malayan race. In this study the word 'Malayan' is used geographically, relating to Malaya (West Malaysia). The word 'Malay' denotes the group of people calling themselves Malay, who are found in lowland and coastal Sumatra, the southern part of the Malay peninsula, and the coastal fringes of Borneo.

Austronesia, a word here used to denote not a state or an empire, but a culture and a period of time, formerly extended deeply into Southern Asia, including the Indo-Chinese peninsula, much of southern China and north-eastern India. The enlargement and expansion of the continental civilizations of the Orient, and in particular the southward expansion of the Chinese culture, which caused large numbers of adjacent people, including the Burmese, the Thai and the Vietnamese, to move south into the Indo-Chinese peninsula, had the effect of submerging Austronesian influence there. Austronesian characteristics are to be found among the present inhabitants of the Indo-Chinese peninsula, notably in Cambodia, but in general these characteristics are so entwined with others derived from further inland that they cannot be separately observed.

Some of the tribal people in Burma, southern China and north-eastern India represent remote enclaves of Austronesian influence, none of them representative subjects for study.[1] The Austronesian civilization was not tribal. Such influence as it had on tribes in Asia – mainly linguistic influence – was peripheral, the tribes in most cases retaining their own culture, which belongs to an earlier, pre-Austronesian period, which will be referred to here as Melanesian.

This last is a word of convenience. The surviving tribes in the areas just mentioned are not Melanesian by race. Their culture, however, modified by continental influences, belongs to that period of prehistoric time which is culturally typified by Melanesia.

Only in the islands of Asia can Austronesian influences and characteristics be isolated and observed. Their endurance there is due to the geographical factor that, these being islands, they were

---

[1] The most interesting of these enclaves is that of the Naga people of north-eastern India. The Naga represent a fusion of Pacific and Asian culture, with particularly strong Pacific elements.

only distantly affected by that prehistoric expansion of continental culture in the Orient from sources inland, which eventually brought continental people to the coasts of Asia, and everywhere altered the pre-existing cultural fabric. Secondly, Austronesian society in Asia was insular, coastal and riverine in nature, always most strongly entrenched on islands.

It is for these reasons that the Austronesian survival line is drawn where it is on the map. Though traces of Austronesia are to be found north and west of the line, it is south and east of it, along a division concerned with men and money, that its existence and nature become apparent.

It is extraordinary that such a division should exist in the Orient, where the laws of economics were being studied and taught before Alexander the Great invaded India. For more than a thousand years the people of Insular Asia have been in contact with the economies of China and India. In their own islands, even in their own small towns and villages, they have for centuries been face to face with Chinese and Indian economic and commercial practices, and later with Arabs as well. Yet of these matters they have learned little or nothing.

The nations of Insular Asia are divided into those in which Chinese and Indians have come in large numbers to small populations, among whom they have so rooted themselves as to be integral to the nation; and those in which, though themselves large in number, they have settled amid populations far larger, among whom they maintain a small, persecuted alienship. In either case they dominate the economy.

Ceylon, population 13,000,000, and Malaysia, population 10,000,000, come into the first category. These are countries in which the non-indigenous are in such numbers as to be found in every level of society from rich to poor, engaged in every kind of activity, many of their poor being poorer than the indigenous.

In the second category come Indonesia and the Philippines.

Indonesia's population now stands around 125,000,000, the world's fifth largest national population, of whom Chinese represent 2.7%. The Chinese control the entire internal economy of the coun-

try, and by various indirect contrivances are the principal beneficiaries of the nation's wealth. In the Philippines, with a population
around 38,000,000, of whom 1.5% are unassimilated Chinese, the
degree of Chinese economic control is less extreme and more indirect, though it is sufficient to be the determining factor in the
nation's economic survival.

Were the Chinese to be flown out of these two countries, both
would relapse within weeks into economic stagnation and chaos,
principally because credit arrangements would break down. The
Chinese, with their understanding of credit, provide a service of
vital importance in Indonesia and the Philippines, countries in
which credit, except in simple forms, such as a landowner advancing
credit to a tenant farmer, is not understood.

Chinese and Indians in these countries seldom extend credit to
the indigenous. They have learned by experience not to. Operating
on credit, the indigenous tend to get into a muddle, and either fold
up or abscond.

These population figures, however, do not tell the whole story.
Every community has its fringes, and the actual number of people
who really control matters is smaller than the figures might suggest.
2.7% of Indonesia's population means there are well over 3,000,000
Chinese in the country. How many of these are sufficiently well off
to pay taxes ?

With this question one draws closer to the truth. As an Indonesian Chinese businessman put it recently: 'In this country of
125,000,000 the entire structure of government, its works and
services, is financed by the taxes, unofficial taxes and bribes paid by
100,000 people.'

The prehistoric civilization of Austronesia, because it had no
handwriting and left no monuments, makes itself known today
through hints, of which the field of study lies in the dual yet indis-
soluble subject of people and language. The inability to understand
money and its utilization is one of these hints. The presence of this
unusual factor in Insular Asia is due to Austronesian reasons.

2 Economy and the Indigenous

The market

Professor Clifford Geertz, in the introduction to his book *The Religion of Java*,[1] has given a classic description of a small-town Javanese market, so accurate that to write another would be work wasted. With his permission it is reproduced here:

> The core of native-run commercial life is the market, where each day hundreds of professional or semi-professional Javanese salesmen and speculators, both men and women, bargain vigorously in a desperate attempt to earn a living or part of a living from small-scale, person-to-person trade. Textiles, daily food supplies, and dry-season crops probably form the bulk of the business; but buttons, dried fish, mats, baskets, perfumes, religious books, cooked food and hot coffee, chairs and tables, nails, ready-made clothing, meat, patent medicines, leather goods, parasols, pots and pans – in fact, almost everything portable – are each day passed from hand to hand to someone's (usually small) profit.
>
> In the market you can have your hair cut, your bicycle fixed, and your pants mended while you wait. For an Indonesian quarter you can rent a spot under a tree or a wooden shed and sell cigarettes for a cent more than you just paid for them in a Chinese store across the street. You can buy a basket of corn[2] in the morning and sell it at noon, never leaving the market – getting your profit out of the slight rise in price which takes place every day as the market wears on. (If you are a friend or a paying acquaintance of the man who runs the scales, you may make something out of the greater weight the corn has when you sell it than when you bought it.) Or, for two rupiahs a day[3] (and a few hundred rupiahs capital), you can become one of the aristocrats of the market with a three-meters wide stall of your own, selling imported and domestic textiles for as much more than they are worth as you can wheedle an unwary

[1] See Bibliography.
[2] Maize.
[3] Less than 4 cents U.S.

peasant into paying. For the Javanese . . ., whether buyer or seller, the market is the very model of commercial life, the source of nearly all his ideas of the possible and the proper in economic behavior.

As will have been deduced, a large part of all the goods sold in this market have been purchased retail from the Chinese shops which are the commercial nucleus of the town. These shops either control, or are linked with, the nearby rice mills and lumber yards, and conduct an important trade in dry-season crops. The Chinese also own all the rickety old transport in the neighbourhood, including all the pedicabs, which they rent out to the indigenous who ply them. The town's cinema is Chinese-owned, as is the theatre where the traditional Javanese plays are performed; Chinese also manage the carnival when it comes to town. In short, nearly everything which makes this town a town is Chinese.

In the midst of all this real-life, down-to-earth Chinese activity sits or squats this unreal, dreamlike market, in which no one ever makes a profit. The minuscule profit made today has to go into a new investment at the Chinese shop tomorrow. In fact, what takes place each day at that market is not trade. It is a kind of ritual – and in this can be detected another hint of the Austronesian past, in which trade was ceremonial, and there was no profit motive.

Note also Professor Geertz's use of the word 'proper'. The market, he says, is the model of everything *proper* in economic behaviour. This is a word of key significance, again with Austronesian undertones. It is not proper, in any given society, such as the temporary society of the market, to trade in such a way as to make undue profit, to be noticeably better off than the seller next to one. A state of social imbalance would thereby be created. Profits, yes – and the haggling that goes on is tremendous. But by the end of the day all the profits made are of more or less similar dimensions, all on the same level. It has been a terrific struggle to achieve even these profits – an equal struggle which brings no social imbalances, however.

Accumulation

Then, how about the man who operates independently, free of the market's innate restrictions ? Surely a man on his own, a man with some talent, could do better than this? Surely he could take the next step, which is to earn enough today to finance himself for two days ahead, instead of one . . .?

Some months ago, at dusk, I was sitting beneath the colonnade of a tumbledown old hotel in Jakarta, capital of Indonesia, when on the other side of the street I noticed a *saté* man fanning his coals. I was with a Singapore Chinese friend, and I suggested we have some *saté*. At our request the *saté* man came over and cooked for us on the colonnade.

While he was cooking, my Chinese friend asked him about the economics of his business. It appeared that he bought two chickens a day for his *saté* sticks, and made a daily profit of Rs. 200 – about 65 cents U.S.

Java is distinguished from end to end by the low standard of food served in public places. It is an island in which, except in a private home, it is very difficult to get a good meal. At a glance we both saw that this man's *saté* was a good deal superior to any we had come across recently. He was a man who could go places, and I could feel my Chinese companion mentally working out how long it would take a Chinese in similar circumstances to quit being mobile and set up a small shop.

'Have you ever made more than Rs. 200 a day?' he asked.

'Never,' the man replied.

Encouragingly, my friend pursued:

'Have you ever tried to make Rs. 500 a day?'

'Never.'

'How about on festival days?'

The *saté* man shook his head with a smile.

'Never,' he replied.

My friend leaned back deeply in his chair, turned to me, and said in English:

'What in heaven's name is one to do with people like this?'

It was a moment of truth, vividly demonstrating the authenticity of that line on the map of the Orient. The human mind in the continental Orient thinks of business in terms of profits that will lead on to increase, as does the Western mind. Money or profit that does not increase is in fact diminishing.

It is true that capital is used to an absurdly small degree in the Orient. The main reason for this is that the joint family system militates against it. Only by resisting the insatiable demands of the joint family – and by being in its members' eyes extremely mean and selfish – can a man accumulate enough to lay the foundations of capital and credit. These foundations, however, are thoroughly understood.

South and east of that line on the map one can temporarily forget about credit and capital. The entry point to these processes is the urge to accumulate, and as demonstrated by the *saté* man, representative of millions, even the entry point is absent. He had absolutely no urge to accumulate. Though he took kindly to my Chinese friend's inquiries about his business, the suggestion that he try to make more money merely struck him as quaint.

Social balance versus *accumulation*

Inevitably there are exceptions to this rule that men do not understand money.

There was a young man who will be called Yakub, who from his schooldays was unusually interested in commerce, believing he could do well in it if he could get a chance. He lived in a *kampong*, a semi-rural Malay settlement on the outskirts of town. The town centre was inhabited and dominated by Chinese, with smaller communities of Indians and Arabs. Virtually no indigenous people lived in the town itself, preferring the outskirts, where they could have their fruit trees and flower gardens, and keep a few chickens. The indigenous, from the earliest descriptions of them, have always had this characteristic of living on the outskirts of towns, rather than in them. Even in the days of the sultanate of Malacca, the wealthiest city in South-East Asia in the fifteenth century, Indians and others lived in the city, the indigenous on the outskirts.

After leaving school Yakub was lucky enough to get a job in a European concern. He was the only person in his *kampong* to have a commercial job in town. In due course he set up a small export business of his own, and purchased a second-hand motorcycle, which he kept underneath his wooden house on stilts in the *kampong*. He was by this time married with a daughter.

Till now, apart from the unusual feature that he was in commerce, he had seemed to his neighbours to be just the same as all of them. The advent of the motorcycle, the only one in the *kampong*, was the first sign that he was perhaps not quite the same as the rest. Nothing was said, and he noticed no change in the way neighbours treated him. In fact, however, the motorcycle was a first sign of social imbalance. One man was ahead of the rest, had *more* than the rest.

Two years later Yakub sold his motorcycle, and bought a very old car, about seventh-hand. Among his commercial friends Yakub's car was a joke, which he cordially shared.

In the *kampong* the car was seen very differently. No one in the *kampong*, or in any other nearby *kampong*, had ever owned a car. Few of them had ever sat in a private car. Social imbalance was now a patent fact.

First, from within the *kampong*, an attempt was made to poison Yakub's wife, the agent being a seemingly friendly woman neighbour, who daily brought dishes in for the wife to savour. This attempt was detected, and failed. Next, a sorcerer was engaged to cast a spell over the wife and children, with intent that they wither away and die. From an outside source this too was discovered. The family's relations with others in the *kampong* being outwardly normal, as if nothing strange was happening, nothing could be said about it.

The attempted poisoning had been worrying enough. The wife, as is often the way with women in these countries, took the spell far more seriously. She went in fear of her life.

The spell had no effect. The next measure taken after this had been observed by the perpetrators was that Yakub's second child, an infant son, was kidnapped. It was cleverly done; all attempts to find the child failed. After four days the boy was returned by a clever device, making it seem he had wandered off into a rival *kampong*, where he had been 'looked after'. But by this time the wife could not stand any more, and told Yakub so.

The cause of all the trouble was the car. Yakub's business, however, had progressed to a point where the car was essential to him. To sell it would mean throwing in his business.

Every *kampong* tends to be a tight social group, often having rivalries with other *kampongs*. It would not be easy to move to another *kampong*. Reluctantly, Yakub and his family moved into rented rooms in a Chinese house in town, where his wife could feel safe. He moved, in other words, into a Chinese urban environment, and remained in it as the only possible means of pursuing his career in peace.

Cases of this kind are rare, but they occur. I can think of three similar instances in other towns where – minus the poison and spells – the same situation arose, with the same outcome.

This is the obverse and sinister side of what British colonial officials despairingly called 'the *kampong* mentality'. Its positive side, which within a community has much to be said for it, is that everyone must live as equals, with a mean standard of wealth. This is what is meant in these societies by social balance.

What is revealed in this is a mentality which expresses itself in the people's *need* for social balance as just defined. Among Indonesians it is not proper – that important word – to be a little better off than your neighbours; and when propriety, as it is understood in these communities, is breached, it creates a *mentally unbearable situation*, in which people will resort to any measures, however evil or silly, to bring things back to what is deemed proper.

Yakub having left, the *kampong* was restored to propriety, and everyone felt at ease again. None from the *kampong* tried to work mischief on him in town. None felt any ill-will towards him. They just thought him strange.

The Philippines' extended family

In the Philippines the problem of men and money is less acute, and less apparent.

When Pacific people first came into Asia, the Philippines were understandably less attractive to them than were Indonesia and the riverine coasts of continental Asia. The seas around the Philippines were unpredictable, while the islands themselves were subject to cyclones (typhoons) and earthquakes. Those who, over the course of centuries, settled in small groups here and there were more of a pioneering type than the rest. The *barangay*, the typical Philippine rustic community, was less concentrated than the Javanese *desa* or the Malay *kampong*, each man in a *barangay* more of an individual, less amenable to control. This general condition was at a later date influenced by historical factors concerned with Chinese and Spaniards.

Adventurous Chinese have been coming in their junks for more than a thousand years to the Philippines, where some have settled and married local girls, their children toning into the landscape. When the Spaniards established themselves in the islands, from 1565 onward, a profitable line of Chinese commerce opened between South China and Luzon, and the age-old gentle admixture of Chinese by assimilation received slightly more impetus. The result today is that many Filipinos, particularly in Luzon, are almost indistinguishable from Chinese, and nearly everyone in the country has some Chinese blood in his veins.

This has produced two effects. Firstly, it has hardened the mental fibre of the Filipinos, making the people more adaptable to circumstances, more resilient. Secondly, it has caused an enlargement of the family unit.

The Chinese did not bring with them the joint family system in an unadulterated form, based as this is on clan. Wherever they settled abroad, the clan ceased to exist as a factor in their lives. Despite escaping from the clan (which was what it amounted to), the Chinese nonetheless felt an emotional need for families with a larger social structure than those they found in Insular Asia.

It is a feature of the islands – a feature which belongs to the Austronesian world – that they did not have the joint family system, but had unit families, more or less the same as those of northern Europe and North America.

In relation to a people who do not understand money, the unit family is a disadvantage. When seeking to raise money to start a business, the first and obvious persons to turn to are one's relatives; and a large family offers more prospects than a small one.

The Chinese emotional need for wide family ramifications caused an extension of family structure in the Philippines, and this process was aided by the happy accident that the Spaniards brought with them Latin ideas about family and, in the Roman Catholic Church, a Latin form of Christianity, with its stress on the big family. It was in fact Spain which provided the key social method to structural extension of families, by bringing the idea of the *compadre* system, whereby families artificially link themselves by godparenthood, thereby often forming large and influential groups.

The end-result does not bear much resemblance to the joint family system. With it came the Christian ethic that a man works for himself and has a right to what he earns, a concept which is foreign to the joint family. But it does mean that a social structure has come into being which, for a people with no inherent understanding of money, offers more likelihood of commercial activity and growth than does the unit family system of Indonesia.

It does not go so far as one might imagine, however, nor so far as would often appear.

Try buying a new set of tyres for your car in Manila, the Philippine capital, and you will be fortunate if you succeed in obtaining them without making a full cash advance. The garage which you ask to supply them will as likely as not be operating without stock and with no command of credit, while the agent and the dealer, seemingly prosperous, will probably be placed likewise; without cash they cannot operate.

The only real beneficiary of commerce such as this is the United States manufacturer. It is in fact the Javanese market in a slightly larger dimension, rendered economically possible by the Philippines' extended family structure. Though capable of expansion, as it expands its stability lessens, and a point is soon reached when, unless invisibly propped up by Chinese or foreign interests, it will collapse.

Caste and language in Ceylon

In Ceylon, among the Singhalese there was a modification of a different kind, which had a similar effect of extending the family structure and conferring more stability.

The degree of prehistoric immigration from India must have been considerable; it clearly began long before the first traditionally recorded influx of 543 B.C. Just as many Filipinos have become indistinguishable from Chinese, so did the Singhalese, though at an earlier date, become virtually indistinguishable from Indians.

Except, of course, in character, as can be seen at once by any visitor passing from South India to Ceylon. The faces on either side of the Palk Strait look the same, but whereas in South India they were mournful and solemn, in Ceylon they are cheerful and one hears laughter. It is an entirely different and more relaxed atmosphere, itself a subtle reminder of the Austronesian character, which everywhere left its imprint.

The extension of family ramifications in Ceylon was due to the fact that with Indians came caste based on a division of human occupations. Within a caste of this kind, inter-family relationships similar to those achieved by the *compadre* system – i.e. not necessarily blood relationships to begin with – become possible.

A highly complex caste system took root in Ceylon. Buddhism, opposed to caste, was unable to dislodge it. The people became Buddhist, but adhered to their castes, which have been strenuously preserved to the present day.

The fact that Singhalese commerce seldom expands beyond the dimensions of a village shop owes largely to lack of attraction for trade or towns. Like all people with a strain of Pacific descent, the Singhalese are pre-eminently country people. Where Filipinos were coerced by Spanish friars into congregating in towns in the better interests of Christian supervision, the Singhalese, with no such experience, remained more rural.

But in general they handle money with more assurance and attention to saving, there is less indebtedness, and among the influential, thanks to family ramifications and cohesion, there is a degree of financial stability rarely found in the Austronesian world.

Another feature is that Austronesian language, which in derivative form was once the speech of Ceylon, was replaced by the parent of present-day Singhalese, derived from Sanskrit.

The Sanskritic languages reflect the mind of man at a more ad-

1. An Indonesian market: fruit and flowers, but no vegetables.

A Pacific atoll, home and origin of the Austronesian civilization.

2. The transferred atoll. *Above:* The skyline trees right and left denote villages in an ocean of rice. *Below:* Sometimes the clumps of trees draw quite near, but they never join, each being a social island.

vanced stage of intellectual development than had been reached at the early epoch reflected in Austronesian language. In Ceylon the adoption of Sanskritic language had the effect of widening the field of human expression, rendering it easier for adaptations to be made.

Over the past centuries innumerable words have been added to the languages of Insular Asia – Sanskrit, Arabic, Portuguese, Spanish and Dutch. The Dutch contribution to Indonesia's national language is in fact the largest ever made by a European language to an Asiatic one. Yet no amount of added vocabulary can alter syntax, which dictates the type of thought formation which is possible in any language. Language is the route to the discovery of Austronesia. It is in addition the restrictive influence without which all trace of it would long since have vanished.

Thus, among the countries of Insular Asia, it is in Indonesia that Pacific traces are to be seen at their clearest. In the Philippines and Ceylon these have been modified, in the former by Chinese and Spanish influences, in the latter by even stronger influences from India.

3 Exploitation

Impotent money

In the Javanese market money was circulating, but in minuscule, in the restricted area of the market. It had no effect on the surrounding countryside, and could cause nothing to develop. Not a single additional wing to a single wooden house would be added as an outcome of it. It had no outcome other than the next meal or two. In this sense it could be called impotent money, circulating impotently.

There are Filipinos who buy a few baskets and other local craft products of Luzon, take a berth in one of the inter-island steamers, and go off for weeks on end, buying local products of one island and selling those of another. It pays for all their expenses, and they lead an interesting life. They never make any money, however.

Trade of this kind sometimes reaches sizeable proportions. The most substantial operators in the region are the Bugis of South Celebes, whose fine two-masted sailing vessels, the Macassar schooners, ply throughout these Eastern waters, even trading at major commercial centres such as Singapore. Operating as cargo carriers, delivering essential supplies such as kerosene to remote islands and small ports off the beaten track of major shipping, with such cash as they obtain from this they buy up local products here, sell them there, buy more local products there, sell them at the next place, and so on interminably. It could be said that they plough their money back into their own industry. Yet they do so without ever making any real profit. Their only capital is their ship, and their house in Celebes.

This is another case of money circulating impotently. Nothing in the Bugis homelands improves or develops.

It might be thought that a man owning valuable cash crops might see things in a different light, and be capable of accumulating some modest capital. In this region the most valuable of all cash crops are spices – cloves, nutmeg and mace, tamarind, cinnamon, candlenuts, saffron, tumeric – the lure which brought the Portuguese, later followed by Spaniards, to make their voyages of discovery, which revealed the world to the world.

The Spice Islands – they are among the world's most beautiful – stretch in the shape of a crescent moon from the Moluccas, through Amboina and Ceram, curving south-westward to Flores and Sumba in the Indonesian archipelago. The southern ones in particular have a pronounced dry season, life is delightfully simple, man's wants are few, and each year there are good profits to be made at the expense of little work. Apart from pepper growing, which is a full-time occupation, spices to a great extent take care of themselves. The trees grow. Their owner merely has to pick the fruits at the right time, and keep his ears open about the price. He may occasionally prune the trees too, if he is fastidious.

Go anywhere in the Spice Islands, however, and observe what happens when word is received that a ship will be loading. Down from the hills comes the grower, with his sacks of cloves and nutmegs laden on his horses. He knows exactly what the price is, and will bargain with the town dealer till he gets it. He will then pay off some debts in town, buy a few necessities and many trivialities, and after losing some money on a cockfight, will mount everything on his horses and go home. The amount of money in his village at dusk will be the same as it was at dawn.

Meanwhile, the dealer is probably also the shipper, and may even be the shipowner as well. Thus the real beneficiary of all this activity is an invisible personage, ethnically Chinese, in Jakarta.

This is what is meant by saying that these countries have an exploitation rather than an economy. There is nothing new about this situation, nor has it anything to do with colonialism. It is a situation which, with variations depending on the type of government in control, has been in existence ever since the Austronesian world encountered trade for profit, a theory which was new to it, and which it has never quite understood.

Money unrelated to time

As a general rule, the people of Insular Asia do not understand the relationship between money and time. They do not have the kind of mind which, on receiving a month's salary, mentally deducts the rent and the electricity bill, divides the remainder by four, and says, 'This means I can spend such-and-such per week.' Money in Insular Asia means money *now*, and before you know where you are it will have been spent.

It is to the salaried that this feature presents the most difficulties, providing society with some of its most obdurate problems. More than any other form of gain, a salary demands attention to money in relation to time. Few employers being prepared to give advances, the salaried person who does not time-space his expenditure is left to fend for himself for part of each month, either by borrowing, or by resorting to corruption or theft.

The number of indigenous people in Insular Asia who understand how to live on a salary is pitifully small. Down the entire hierarchy of salarydom, from army generals to municipal dustmen, most are either in debt, or struggling to keep going till the next paycheck by practising various forms of corruption, the lower-paid often on a deplorably small and humanly degrading scale. Where salaries are inadequate, this is reflected in general corruption affecting cities and nations. Where salaries are commensurate with needs, the corrupting effect which the salaried have on society lessens in degree.

It remains, however. No matter how high the salary paid to people who do not understand the relation between money and time, toward the end of the third week of the month money will be running short.

The morally upright who are proud of their jobs stick it out, often going short of food for a time each month in a desperate endeavour to keep themselves from sinking deeper into debt. This naturally is reflected in their work. In any Insular Asian organization in which indigenous people work on salaries, it will be found that at certain times of the month, depending on whether they are paid weekly, fortnightly or monthly, listlessness descends on them, during which they do no real work.

Where regular work is concerned, many of the uneducated are

virtually unemployable. On receiving their paychecks they are not seen again for several days. It is not that they have got drunk – drunkenness is not a feature of Insular Asia. Somehow, with money in hand, they have been having a pleasant time, and with one thing and another they only turn up again for work when there is no money left.

The majority of fishermen in Insular Asia only go to sea when they have no more money. If they have a good catch and the price is good, they stay ashore longer. As a result, they are among the poorest. Where cooperative societies have been introduced as a means of improving their lot, these have had little effect. Though a well-run cooperative might send up profits, with money spent and work done in the immemorial way the adverse monsoon came each year to find the fishermen penniless – obliged to obtain rice on credit to tide them over the months when fishing is impossible.

The principle of time-spaced expenditure and saving can naturally be explained to people, and it often is. In addition, many universities run economics courses. Yet somehow principle is seldom put into practice. The truth is that among many there is a preconceived sense of inability to handle money in a stable and productive way, a feature to which the fatalism of Islam has contributed, being most pronounced in Muslim communities.

When sickness strikes and there is no money to pay for medicines or a doctor, people resignedly accept premature or needlessly painful death. When school fees have to be paid and there is no money, children who went to school for a term or two go no more.

Money in Insular Asia means money *now*, and in an unexpected way nature herself has conspired to accentuate this.

The ricefields of Java are a sight no one can ever fail to marvel at, agriculturally one of the most impressive sights the world has to offer. In a single vista one sees waterlogged ploughing in one field, the brilliant green of a nursery in another, elsewhere rows of men engaged in the second planting, everywhere rice in all stages of growth, in every colour from dark green to shimmering gold; and beside it there are dry fields of stubble, and the cheerful piles of stacked ears waiting to be carried to the village.

Spring, summer, autumn and winter all at once, and it has been thus for centuries. The Javanese would not understand the patience of farmers in other parts of the world, who must wait so long for their crops to mature, and must sow with such attention to the season. In country life in Java, home of 95,000,000 people, there is no necessity to think in such terms, no need to calculate in weeks or months. All is present. Money means *now*. So is it with rice. Rice is *now*, eternally so. Wherever one looks, there is harvesting going on somewhere, the everlasting harvest of today.

Such conditions provide an important factor in the time–money relationship problem.

PART II

The Transferred Atoll

On sent dans cette race quelque chose d'humain,
de sensé, de sociable et de poli qui date de loin.

ERNEST SABATIER: *Sous l'équateur du Pacifique*

4 The Transferred Atoll

Approximately 4,500 miles east of Java lie the Gilbert Islands. Dead flat, not visible to one another, they lie in the lonely infinity of ocean, just west of the intersection of the equator and the international date line. There are sixteen of them, and they are atolls.

The society of an atoll was the predominant and characteristic social formation of the prehistoric Austronesian civilization. In order to understand the countries of Insular Asia, which are contemporary survivals of the Austronesian world, it is necessary to begin by studying certain aspects of society on an atoll, and the way of life there.

The reason that the Gilbert Islands have been selected for this purpose from among the myriad atolls and islands of the Pacific is, firstly, because these are the most classic of atolls, presenting atoll conditions in an extreme and classic form, and secondly (more importantly in relation to this study), the people are closer than any others, racially and culturally, to those who voyaged and traded in the great days of the Austronesian world. The Gilbertese have preserved characteristics which elsewhere in the Pacific have been altered by later events, themselves also prehistoric. This applies to nearly all Polynesia, which today reflects the people and society of a later date, which could be called post-Austronesian.

In the Gilberts one is face to face with real antiquity, a living contact with an ancient world of refinement and eminence. As anyone will know who has visited them, the Gilbert Islands are the very core, the inner soul of the Pacific.[1]

The nature of an atoll
An atoll is a coral organism lying exactly at the surface of ocean,

---

[1] The distinguished Pacific scholar H. E. Maude has described them as 'unique – the ultimate citadel-heart of Oceania'. See Rosemary Grimble, *Migrations, Myth and Magic from the Gilbert Islands*.

where air and water meet, which are the only conditions in which coral can live. The coral is in the shape of a ring, and encloses a staggeringly beautiful emerald-green lagoon.

Each atoll is the topmost point of a submarine pillar of limestone extending several thousand feet down into the depths of the ocean, where it is impregnably attached to the crater of a long-extinct volcano which was once, millions of years ago, at sea level, and which has very slowly sunk. As it sank, the coral which had formed round it struggled for survival at water-level by building new cells on top of the submerging old ones, which died and, due to the sea's action, became solid limestone of enormous strength. The pillar on which each atoll rests represents millions of years of this process.

Over these millions of years, *débris* drifting in from the ocean on the windward side (south-east) has caused a small strip of land to form, nowhere more than eight feet high, and in some places so narrow that one could shoot an arrow from the lagoon beach on one side to the ocean beach on the other. Amid these strips of land are small and very precious deposits of cultivable soil.

Each atoll, impregnable and self-protecting, offers complete safety to human life, provided enough food can be scraped together; and the Gilbert Islands seem at all times in their long past to have supported a teeming population relative to the size of their habitable area, which by continental, or even by average insular standards, is microscopic.

These are, in relation to land, the smallest human habitations in the world, a factor which affects the way people there live and think.

Take an English village in the Cotswolds and lift it up, just its houses and gardens, with no fields or any communications, and set it down on a piece of land exactly the same size, surrounded on all sides by a thousand miles of oceanic emptiness. The social arrangement of life in that village, with no fields, no cows or sheep, no contact with any other village or town, no means of marrying except within the village, and no way of escape from the consequences of a bad deed, would undergo profound changes, producing a different kind of society – unless, of course, in frustration, the people killed each other, as they almost certainly would.

This, it could be said, was life on a limited scale; and to it nature has imposed her own set of limitations. Very few things will grow on a Gilbert atoll. The earth in the strips of land contains salt and lime to a degree which little in nature can stand. The coconut will grow, though the coconut water tastes slightly salt. The pandanus grows, and is the people's most important tree, used for house and boat construction, baskets, mats, string and gum; and it has edible fruit. Breadfruit will grow, but it fruits erratically. Bananas will grow in some places, but they are of poor quality. Apart from this, there are one or two small equatorial bushes, including a mangrove, and some flowering bushes, which include hibiscus, the bark of which was used in the making of wearing apparel. Beaten out with a coral mallet, it becomes soft and fine, somewhat resembling kidskin.

Only one vegetable, the Polynesian taro, known as *babai*, will grow; and this is cultivated with the greatest care in the small, precious deposits of cultivable soil, *babai* being of special importance because in the people's diet it stands in lieu of cereal. Breadfruit is also a substitute cereal, but because it cannot be relied on to fruit, it is of less importance than *babai*.

These days, of course, imported rice and potatoes are available. For the purposes of this study, what has happened since Westerners came to the Pacific must be ignored, consideration being given solely to conditions as they were prior to that date.

Magic and incentive

The cultivation of *babai* had a sacred character, connected with magic.

Magic, in its original and purest sense, is the relating of thought to action, or more specifically, the relating of the human will to action. Behind it stands the theory that human action on its own, combined with such thought as a carpenter takes before sawing a piece of wood, is well enough in its way. It may turn out to be successful. It has far more likelihood of being successful, however, if behind it there is the human will to make it succeed.

The human will is psychic, deriving its strength from the intangible. Before undertaking an important action, by drawing on the intangible the human will is strengthened, making the outcome surer of success.

There is nothing uncivilized or primitive about magic. Everyone knows the man with a will to succeed, and how he usually does succeed. Magic in Austronesia was the practical expression of a philosophy similar to this, except that it was conscious, formal, and often ritualistic.

Where the ancient world of the Pacific differed from ours was in its lack of incentive. Incentive on an atoll – remember the English village transferred there – is non-existent. But in magic, intimately related to man as far back as he can be traced, he had a built-in incentive system, relating to all his important actions.

Thus, when it is said that the cultivation of *babai* was sacred, it has to be understood in this dual sense, for which there is no equivalent in modern terms. *Babai* was not cultivated *because* it was sacred, nor was it sacred *because* it was cultivated. It was cultivated because it was important. Being important, activity connected with it demanded to a high degree the application of the human will.

Cultivation of *babai* was a man's occupation. Since the work is not unduly arduous – it simply demands regular attention – it would be tempting to imagine a division of labour, wherein men engaged in the more arduous and dangerous job of fishing, while women looked after the *babai*. Nothing like this happened. Men took charge of both occupations, for reasons concerned with *mana*.

Mana – in the Gilberts the word actually used is *maka* – is the soul or spirit energy in physical things, the intangible, energizing quality which causes a seed to put forth a shoot and roots, all physical life being inseparable from an intangible, or psychic element. All things possess *mana* in varying degree, meaning that *mana*, the intangible, expresses itself through them. Men, being more energic than women, possess more *mana* than any other living thing. *Babai*, being the staple food, the upholder of life, is strong in *mana*, and needs to be handled by men, strongest of all in *mana*, and thus the most fitted to animate, or clinch with, the *mana* in *babai*, causing it to grow well.

Here, then, is a community who live largely on fish, which is varied and plentiful. They live surrounded by coconuts and some fruit trees. Though they give great attention to cultivating their substitute cereal, they have no other forms of cultivation, none being possible.

It was noted earlier how Malays, living in their *kampongs* on the outskirts of towns, had their fruit trees and flower gardens, while nothing was said about vegetables. This is a feature which is found all over that region.

In Indonesia today, in the neighbourhood of large cities, there is commercial vegetable cultivation, nearly always invisibly organized and controlled by Chinese. But go out into the rural heart of Java, and it will be found that, while the greatest attention is given to rice, the cereal and staple, the only vegetables to be found are those that have seeded themselves – chillies, long beans and pumpkins, with any luck. There is nowhere a tradition of vegetable cultivation.

Moreover, in Java there is little or no idea of relating vegetables to other food. A plate of rice and dried fish will be served, and beside the rice will be placed a red chillie, at which one nibbles if one dares, in an endeavour to give the food some taste. The presence of chillies, beans and pumpkins makes one aware that one is no longer on a Gilbert atoll. But one almost might be.

And just as the cultivation of *babai*, the substitute cereal, is a sacred occupation, so among Indonesians there is a sacred character in respect of the cereal, rice. Throughout these lands only men plant the seeds of rice, for the same ancient reasons as obtained on the atolls, usually explained today in Insular Asia by the casual informa-tion that men are stronger, though actually meaning that they are stronger in *mana*, or *semángat*, as this word becomes in Indonesia.

Neither Islam nor Christianity has had any effect on this deep-rooted Austronesian concept. At harvest time a special little knife is used (again by men) with great attention to cutting the ear of rice in such a way as not to damage the spirit of life (*semángat*) in it. As in the Gilbert Islands, so in Indonesia, such a degree of attention to magic – the mother of incentive, and link between physical and intangible – applies only to the cereal.

Social balance versus *accumulation*

If human beings are to live on anything so small and remote as an atoll, it goes without saying that the laws of behaviour must to a peculiar degree be geared to avoid discontent. We of the West know in our own lives the human stresses, aggressions, and abnormalities caused by overcrowding. The Gilbertese, living in densely crowded conditions, have been successfully dealing with these human problems for many thousands of years.

Nor are they a docile people. Their gentle manners and pithy humour often conceal the fact that they are by nature obstinate and argumentative. Though a Gilbertese is slow to lose his temper, if he does it is serious; while any for whom he may conceive a grudge has grounds for watching out. This latter trait, incidentally, is found throughout Insular Asia, except in Ceylon and among tribal people.

On anything as small as an atoll, land is the most likely source of discontent. Every adult man on a Gilbert atoll owns land, at least in theory, a condition essential to peace and order. At the time of the last conquest many of the defeated took to their boats and were never heard of again, a common feature of Oceanic war. Those who remained forfeited their land to the conquerors, and became slaves. Over the centuries that followed, most of their descendants succeeded in acquiring land. The principle is clear, though. On an atoll one is either a landowner or a slave.

Land matters are rendered doubly serious by the fact that a Gilbertese has really nowhere else to go. If he accidentally drifts on to another Gilbert atoll, he will with luck be looked after, and succeed in returning safely. But if he gets lost at sea, and reaches an atoll in another group, he is liable to be enslaved. (This refers to conditions prior to the last century.) A similar condition arises when a serious crime is committed. The criminal has no real escape. Though knowledge of this acts as a deterrent to serious crime, it does not entirely prevent it.

To a peculiar degree every man is confined to his own tight little society, a human condition which is only just mentally bearable. The least upset in social balance within that community, and a mentally unbearable situation – a phrase encountered before – will have been created.

Should one man, by clever contrivances, acquire considerably more land than others, should he own more boats than others (probably meaning he is more industrious), or, worst of all, should he in a disguised way seek to employ others, conditions will rapidly go beyond the point which the atoll community can stand. A mentally unbearable situation will have been created, in which there is no alternative for the offender (the man who was going up in the world) but to clear out. And where to, one may ask?

Remembering Yakub and his car, it will be seen that his *kampong*, in its ideas of social balance, was the same as a Gilbert atoll. Apart from the fact that it spoke a different, though related, language, his *kampong* was in every other respect a Gilbert atoll picked up and put down in Asia, in a land area to which the tight conditions of an atoll do not apply, but to which the people have not adapted. Though they and their ancestors had undoubtedly been living for centuries amid the lush wealth of Insular Asia, they were still thinking and behaving atoll-wise. Having lost all knowledge of their past, they were unaware of this, but 'the *kampong* mentality' is really the atoll mentality, preserved like a mummy in a land area, to which it is not only irrelevant, but inhibitive to all material advance.

On an atoll an up-and-coming young man is restricted in his avenues of self-expression to the accumulation of possessions. It is to these that one of the atoll's strictest conventions applies. Should a young man accumulate far more sharks' teeth than anyone else, and these be considered desirable objects, any of his kinsmen is at liberty to come and *baboose* one from him.

Baboose, to rhyme with goose, is actually spelt *babuti* in Gilbertese, due to a pedantic orthography conferred on the language by the American missionary Hiram Bingham, Jr., at the turn of this century. The word is pronounced *baboose*, and will be referred to thus.

It means give, borrow, lend, share, part with, or anything else of this kind, with the word *must* attached to it. Ordinary words for borrow, lend and give exist; when they are used, it is up to the solicited to consent or refuse. When the word *baboose* is used – it will be used only by a kinsman – one must give up to him the object *baboosed*.

This is one of the rare aspects of Gilbertese life which can be seen more clearly in reference to the present day than to pre-nineteenth-century conditions.

Among seventy fairly large families there may be six men working abroad. These six will be earning only modest wages, but this is money beyond the wildest dreams of anyone who stays at home on an atoll. When one of them returns from Sydney, he may bring three new pairs of shoes, two transistor radios, four electric torches, ten new shirts and much else besides. Some of it is intended as presents for friends and relatives; the rest, in any ordinary society, would be for himself.

Now, if each of the six returned, and kept most of what he had brought with him, he and others like him would inevitably come to form an upper class based on wealth and outside experience. They would assuredly be in and out of each other's houses, having experience in common and a common interest in safeguarding their property. They would certainly come to exercise influence in atoll affairs, and if they and others like them were to stand together they might well create a plutocracy.

Atoll social convention renders this all but completely impossible. A returnee from Sydney begins by bringing his things home. His intention was to give one of his transistor radios to a friend, keeping the other one for himself. Within hours, he visits his friend and makes his gift. Before dusk, however, a kinsman, calling on the returnee and spying the other radio, has *baboosed* it. The returnee is left with none. Next day some other kinsman will *baboose* a pair of shoes, and within the ensuing days all the electric torches will have gone similarly. In fact, by the end of ten days it would be quite on the cards for the returnee to be left with nothing but one shirt out of all the things he brought. He will be left as poor as he was on the day he went abroad to work.

Due to the intensely constricted life on an atoll, jealousy is more easily inflamed there than in any other kind of society, and among none can its effects prove so lethal. A returnee causes no jealousy. By a strange and ancient method, his possessions have been distributed among quite a number of people; and when one reflects that the same thing has happened to the other five returnees, it can be seen that the convention has the effect of ensuring to everybody a certain mean standard of wealth, which is vital on an atoll if there is not to be trouble.

This is the source of the mental *need* for social balance observed in Insular Asian village life. Transmitted across thousands of years, it stems from the atoll.

What on an atoll is a social necessity, though, in a land area is less so. In the plains of Java there are wider land horizons. A man can escape the consequences of a bad deed by leaving his community, and going to a town. Should a man become wealthier than others, this should in theory be of long-term advantage to a village. It is not seen thus, however.

The transferred architecture of society

The trouble here is that when the atoll people came and settled in Insular Asia, they did not care for the various communal forms of dwelling they found there – longhouses, etc. They constructed their joint place of residence on the only model they knew, the model of an atoll. A typical Javanese village is not only mentally like an atoll; it is an actual physical reproduction of one, surrounded by land instead of water. Though one village may even be within hailing distance of another, each is constituted and constructed as a complete, inward-looking, self-sufficient group, which is what an atoll is and has to be.

In some places the physical resemblance between the two is striking. In the ricelands of Java an ocean of green extends for miles in every direction. Here and there, dotted among it, are clumps of trees, each clump on its own, isolated from any other clump, each entirely surrounded by ricefields. Each of these clumps of trees denotes the presence of a village, though in the entire landscape there is not a house to be seen. All are built within the shelter of the trees, as on an atoll.

Each clump, seen in the distance, looks dense and bushy until one is within it, when, as on an atoll, one discovers its light and airy shade, like a small park, with the earth immaculately swept and smooth to walk on barefoot, the houses occurring as they will, in no special order.

Once within these trees, one realizes that a Javanese village, like an atoll, is an inward-looking society. Look outward, and there is nothing but the eternal ocean – sea-water or rice, as the case may be – and far on the horizon another clump of trees. Whether in a canoe on the ocean, or barefoot along the slippery bunds of the *sawah*, it is a tedious business to reach those other trees. One does it sometimes – at weddings, for instance – but not often. The first time I landed on a Pacific atoll I was immediately reminded of a Javanese village. The resemblance is uncanny. In the ricelands of Java an Austronesian people have by accident of nature been able to model their life in a land area reproducing every essential feature of life in the Pacific Ocean.

The fate of a Gilbert Islander, working hard and buying things to take home, all to no purpose of personal gain, throws light on the lack of urge to accumulate in Insular Asia. All along, the Gilbertese *knew* while working abroad that in the end it could bring him no personal gain. He did not even associate work with gain, or accumulation, no such outcome being possible. He worked because this kept him going from day to day – and of course, too, his return home bearing so many possessions would be a moment of personal glory.

Bearing in mind that it is these anterior conditions which have influenced much of Insular Asia, the attitude of the *saté* man in Jakarta, with no will to make more money, becomes more understandable. His background, stretching back thousands of years, as all human backgrounds do, arises amid a set of basic factors in which personal accumulation did not and could not exist.

The Austronesians, despite having lived for many centuries in Asia, have made surprisingly few adaptations to it. Certain adaptations they have made undeniably. They have taken to growing rice, for instance, instead of their former root crops. The bulk of the adaptations needed in the present age still lie ahead of them.

Here the major obstacle is the village which is constituted on the model of an atoll. Unless this form of construction, inseparable from the way of life that goes with it, can be broken up and dispersed, it is difficult to see how any of the necessary adaptations can be made. And this would only be the first step on a long journey.

The transferred cuisine—Indonesia

Cooking, indeed everything to do with the preparation of food, is of a lower standard in Indonesia than in any other part of the Orient. It is of such a low standard, in fact, as to provide an arresting contrast. Not only do the general run of people not know how to cook, or have only a rudimentary knowledge; in addition, they do not know when to kill an animal, how to select meat, or how to cut it, nor do they know how to flavour meat and fish in the cooking.[1]

The place where one becomes most forcefully aware of the strangeness of this is Jogjakarta, in Central Java, culturally the capital of Indonesia. Jogjakarta is a fine town, nobly laid out, dominated by the Sultan's *kraton*, with the wide processional avenue of Malioboro leading to it. In the environs are two of Asia's most celebrated medieval monuments, the elegant complex of Hindu shrines at Prambánan, perhaps the most beautiful of all Hindu monuments, and the massive and imposing Buddhist sermon in stone, Borobudur. Within the town are many other interesting monuments; it is a place where one walks with history. It is moreover a town of more than 3,000,000 inhabitants. Yet the food there is worse than in any large town in East Asia.

This is doubly remarkable when seen in the light of history. Jogjakarta is one of the Orient's major centres of culture and civilization. It is less known, and has been less esteemed, than some of the others. In fact, it has to be seen in the same rank as Hangchow, Kyoto, Lucknow and Agra.

---

[1] There is one special exception to this. The Minahassa, the horizontal northern arm of the strange-shaped island of Celebes, has a cuisine of its own, derived from local, Filipino, Chinese and Dutch sources. Favourite dishes include field rat and monkey, and as a cuisine it is thus somewhat *recherchée*. The Minahassa, however, is so unusual that it has to be treated as culturally separate from Indonesia in a number of respects, of which this is one.

Cities of this kind, which have experienced centuries of culture, have three special features in common. Firstly, everyone down to the most ordinary railway porter has good manners, with much consideration for others. Secondly, everyone high and low speaks their language clearly and accurately, using a wider vocabulary than elsewhere. Thirdly, each of such cities has its own special and superior cuisine, which will be found to include many old dishes not to be had elsewhere. Even the sweetmeats one buys on the streets of Lucknow are superior to those anywhere else in that part of India.

In Jogjakarta one finds the first and second of these features: manners and good speech. But where is the cuisine? This is a centre of civilization. One is faced not simply by a people with only rudimentary knowledge of cooking, so much as with a civilization in which the culinary art was all but a total blank.

In the homes of the educated – and how many of them are there? – food is of course tasty. All the best dishes, though, are of either Chinese or Dutch invention. One searches in vain for an indigenous cuisine.

At Padang, on the south-western coast of Sumatra, there is a tradition of cookery which has made a name elsewhere, and which appears at first sight to be Indonesian. But why Padang, of all places? When one reflects that Padang has been a place of Chinese settlement for more than three centuries, it occurs as probable that the Padang style of cookery was a joint venture. This probability tends to receive confirmation if one tries Padang food in Jogjakarta where, cooked by Javanese, it has been rendered uneatable by the well-intentioned who do not understand meat preparation or cooking.

Perhaps only those who have lived in the continental Orient can appreciate how strange this is.

In the Pacific, prior to the coming of Europeans, bringing their stoves and kerosene, there was not much cooking done on an atoll. People ate their fish raw, as is widely done to this day. Men just bite the head off, and eat the rest. Octopus, squid and other products of the lagoon were also taken raw. Some marine products were taken sun-dried.

There are no edible wild birds in the atolls; they are too far away; the birds have never found them. Frigates and other sturdy sea-birds are sometimes to be seen, but they would have to be speared, and it is difficult to come close enough to them for this. Archery never developed on atolls, there being nothing from which to make a bowstring.

For much of the time *babai* and breadfruit were the only things cooked. Pigs and chickens (scrawny and sub-standard due to lack of suitable nourishment) are to be found, but pigs would only be cooked for feasts.

Cooking was done in earth-sunken ovens filled with dead coral heated till white-hot. Food on this could be grilled or, wrapped in leaves, baked. No other form of cooking is practicable, and of course there were no seasonings or condiments.[1]

When Pacific people came to Insular Asia, they thus had only a rudimentary cuisine, a striking fact when compared with their music and dancing, which were highly developed, and their know-ledge of astronomy, which was first-rate by any standards. In Java today there is the parallel: a rudimentary cuisine, which comes as a surprise when seen against the setting of Java's high development of music and the arts, and the tremendous popular interest in these. This is another instance where adaptation to a land area has been slight.

Things might have turned out differently had the atoll people discovered a reasonably developed cuisine in Java and other islands. But they did not.

Tradition states that, in man's early days, Java was a grassy island, with virtually no agriculture or domesticated animals. Such people as lived there had a culture similar to Melanesian and Dayak.

What this means in terms of cooking is amply reflected to this day in the remoter parts of the Melanesian and Dayak world, where a chicken is cooked by dropping it dead, feathers and all, into a pot of hot water. The atoll people found a culture which, where cooking

---

[1] Rosemary Grimble, *op. cit.*, p. 121, gives full details of atoll cooking, with an illustration of an oven, explaining how it is heated.

was concerned, was in no way superior to their own, while in other respects the culture was inferior, or so it seemed to them.

The atoll people came to Insular Asia as a people much superior to those they found there. Having nothing to learn from such people, their own culture tended to adhere to the patterns it had already formed in the Pacific. There was no need for them to adapt much. They were confronted with no cultural challenge which, had one existed, might have stimulated them to think things out anew.

Their cooking remained rudimentary.

Yet how was it that at a later date India, with its elaborate cuisine, did not fill this gap in what was otherwise becoming a rich and remarkable culture? This significant omission in Indian influence, otherwise considerable and penetrating, stems from the fact that only Indian *men* came to Java, and Indian men, professional cooks apart, do not and cannot cook. In most of India a man is not even allowed inside a kitchen. Thus while, as tradition states, the Indians introduced chillies, new strains of rice, the domesticated buffalo, irrigation, etc., they could not teach the Javanese how to improve their cooking.

Culinary improvements did not begin to come in till there were resident Chinese in the islands, and later the Dutch. These improvements, however, only affected a small number of the well-to-do. For the rest, food preparation and cooking remained much as they were.

This is an example, one of several, in which it can be observed how, by accident, a cultural pattern has passed from a remote antiquity directly into the modern world, experiencing the changes of the times, yet without colliding with anything capable of altering it.

An unusual phenomenon, it is providential when dealing with a prehistory devoid of monuments and handwriting. Had history caused the atoll-transferred culture of Insular Asia to collide with something capable of radically altering it, this would almost certainly have erased the vital point of contact between a Javanese village and a Pacific atoll, thereby plunging Insular Asia's past into inexhumable obscurity.

The transferred cuisine—the Philippines

In the Philippines, thanks to Chinese influence and intermarriage, a cuisine developed, based largely on that of eastern Kwangtung. Here there was the difference that every Chinese man can cook. With the Chinese, too, came vegetable cultivation, though on what in China would be considered a reduced scale.

At a good Filipino meal, therefore, nearly all the dishes are of Chinese origin. Anyone who has tasted those dishes in their original form in China, however, will at once notice a difference. Each dish, as prepared in the Philippines, is gentler in taste. The sharpness, some of the kick, has gone out of it. This is a faraway harkback to the atoll people.

The tastelessness of atoll food has to be experienced; it cannot be imagined. Gilbertese food surpasses all others in this respect. The food is not in the least unpleasant; it just lacks savour to an extraordinary degree. There is no salt on an atoll, yet everything, even coconut water, tastes slightly salt. This gives a peculiar sameness of taste to everything eaten.

Babai, the only vegetable that will grow, is the most tasteless member of the taro family. A small *babai* has a slight taste, but the root being grown in lieu of a cereal, the aim is naturally to grow them as large as possible, thereby reducing such meagre taste as they possess to near-zero. Eating a large Gilbertese *babai* is the nearest thing imaginable to indulging in the taste of nothing.

To this it must be added that even ocean fish in the neighbourhood of the Gilberts has curiously little taste. A traditional Gilbertese feast is an enormity (because people eat a lot) of good and well-prepared tastelessness.

The sense of taste is transmitted from generation to generation with more persistence than most of man's traits. Every human being, at some time or other, craves for food as he tasted it when he was a child, and with age this craving is apt to increase. Thus the transmission of a sense of taste, though passed essentially from mother to child, is often abetted and reinforced by a parallel transmission from grandparent to grandchild. It is a particularly strong continuity.

In the Philippines, atoll taste encountered Chinese dishes which human craving for childhood food deemed too tasty. Though the dishes were undeniably good, they were modified, making them gentler – less tasty, in fact – bringing them closer to the tastes of childhood inherited through immemorial generations. In this study this is only a small point, but it is a subtle and fascinating one.

Another is the use of taro and other root crops – originally the cereal – in traditional Filipino food. This is seldom to be had in Manila; among old-style country families it is a noticeable feature. The general gentleness of taste at such a meal, together with the use of taro and other roots, immediately evokes, to anyone who knows the atolls of the Pacific, the taste of food there, which still to this day slightly and distantly dictates.

Time on an atoll

The Gilbert Islands lie in the relatively narrow equatorial belt which is unaffected by cyclones. There are no high winds, no dangerous high tides, no storms. Rain comes in pleasant showers throughout the year, more on some atolls, less on others. In addition, being on the equator, there are no seasons. Each day is the same length, experienced in climatic conditions of complete regularity. The weather conditions, in fact, are perfect, eternally so.

This will explain what was meant by these being classic atolls. The other classic and extreme feature is that less will grow in the Gilberts than in many another atoll, where due to different conditions there is slightly more variety of growth, though not much.

Though there were ways of telling the time of day, in daily life the measure of time which people noted most was high and low tide, which on an atoll means the filling and emptying of the lagoon. The only other measure of time recognized was concerned with seasons.

Though the Gilbert Islands themselves have no seasons, the ocean around them has what are in effect seasons. In the course of a year there are two submarine 'seasons', during which various ocean fish turn poisonous. Thus when fishing at sea it was important to know the 'season', indicating which fish to land if caught, and which to throw back into the sea.

These seasons were determined by the position of the Pleiades in relation to Antares, these occupying key positions in Oceanic astronomy. This is a feature of Oceanic knowledge which the Austronesians brought with them into Insular Asia, and disseminated wherever they went. To this day the Land Dayaks, deep in the jungles of Borneo, determine when to sow their hill rice by the position of the Pleiades, a survival from the long-lost Austronesian world.

The atoll people were not geared to time in the same way others are. When they came to Insular Asia, they brought their own mental gearing with them; and in some places nature conspired with them, producing conditions in which seasons, though they exist in a moderate way, are irrelevant to sowing and harvesting. In Java a man may sow rice in one field in the morning, and harvest rice in another field in the afternoon.

It was mainly in relation to agriculture that our minds acquired their gearing to time, which they later came to exhibit in relation to all other occupations. Agriculture, for millions of people in Insular Asia, had no such effect. Here can be seen another of those strange instances in which a trait of human thinking, in this case an important one, has been enabled to slip through from prehistory to the present without colliding with anything capable of altering it.

Time unrelated to work or money

Babai cultivation differed from other work on a Gilbert atoll, in that it demanded fairly regular attention. Other work was done at random.

This does not, however, mean that men most of the time sat around doing nothing. Most of the time most men were working, often with diligence and skill. There was little time, indeed, for sitting around. Boats, sails, fish-hooks and sharktooth spears were having constantly to be made, houses repaired and built; and to make anything on an atoll was a major undertaking, demanding prodigious lengths of patient, steady labour.

Boats, for instance, were all the time ageing and in need of replacement. Assuming that a man possessed the coral pins and planes needed to start with – each of them the product of days and days of industry – it would take at least a week of uninterrupted work to fashion a single plank; and uninterrupted work was seldom possible, what with fishing and social engagements connected with the feasts and song-and-dance festivals which made atoll life interesting. It would probably have taken at least two months to have the planks ready for even the smallest and simplest Gilbertese V-shaped sailing craft.

Then holes had to be bored through the planks with coral pins, another slow, patient undertaking, enabling the planks to be lashed together with tightly coiled tree fibres and gum from pandanus sap. Making the mast and outrigger with coral implements would also have taken several weeks or months.

Meanwhile there was the daily fishing in the lagoon and occasional trips to sea, the *babai* garden to be looked after, dance rehearsals to be attended, new songs to be learned by heart, magic ceremonies to be performed to assure the success of the new boat, and youngsters to be trained in the martial arts. All in all, it was similar to the occasions when we say, 'I was so busy I didn't even notice what the time was; I didn't have time to think'.

This, in fact, was precisely it. There was so much going on in life that there was no time to think about time. Though one worked, often very hard, it was work unrelated to time. And though as often as not it was constant work, it was not what could be called regular work. One did not work by hours. One worked because something had to be done. When it was done, one could perhaps stop and have a rest, till something else had to be done. And of course it was work entirely unrelated to money.

With the coming of Europeans and nails, the bottom fell out of this world. The nail was its disaster. What had formerly taken months could now be done in minutes. A weird transformation took place. The atoll, once a hive of industry, became a place in which for nine-tenths of the day there is nothing to do. There is nothing to do, of course, because on an atoll there are so few *things* to do things with.

Next came other manufactured goods. Where people once made their own clothes, sails and fish-hooks, these could now be imported.

To buy them, however, money was needed. This meant working for money, something hitherto unknown. This in turn meant – equally unknown – regular work.

This last proved to be a serious stumbling block. Regular work seemed to be a system devoid of reason. Doing a job on a basis of hours drained work of all vitality and excitement. It was simply not a man's life. It was boring, and this was reflected in the quality and quantity of work done, giving the people of the Pacific the reputation of being incurably lazy.

This, before the coming of nails, in the days when work was unrelated to time, was the very last thing they were. But in parts of the Pacific, even after a century of experience, people have not adapted to the idea of regular work. Such is the strength of inherited traits in the human mind.

Remembering the Insular Asian fishermen who did not put to sea again till they had spent all their cash – i.e. until there was a *necessity* for going to sea – it can be seen how in terms of atoll culture their attitude is suddenly understandable. An element of their culture has slipped through from prehistory into the modern world without a collision. Though they have learned the relationship between work and money (this is seldom difficult), they have not related money to time.

Ceremonial trade and its motives
Money existed on the atolls. It was manufactured from shells. This work being intricate and delicate, it was usually done by women. Shell money is still manufactured in the Solomon Islands. The pieces, cunningly and attractively wrought, can be strung together like Chinese cash.

Today it has a cash value (one standard-size string is worth two Australian dollars); in ancient times it did not. Though money was highly esteemed, and considered a desirable possession, its value was a prestige value. To some extent it ranked as an *objet d'art*. Because, like everything else, it could be *baboosed*, it was impossible to accumulate large quantities of it individually, though an atoll community which jointly possessed a lot of money would consider itself superior to another community which possessed less. It was used as an item in trade between atolls and groups, but not in the same way money is used today. One did not buy things with it. In ancient Oceanic trade there was no buying or selling.

There seems at all times to have been a great deal of trade in the Pacific, in striking contrast with today, when it is the world's most tradeless region. Since an atoll produces very few things, and each atoll produces more or less the same things, it was trade in variants of the same commodities.

A contemporary example of this kind of trade is Europe's industry in men's ties, in which in any large city the ties of five or so nations will be found vying with each other, little to choose between any of them, yet each enjoying varying degrees of prestige. One may compliment an Englishman on his tie. 'Glad you like it,' he replies; 'it's Italian.' And he derives a certain allure thereby. Similarly, most of the best tie shops in Paris have Scottish or English names, thereby conferring allure on those who buy there. Trade in variants of the same commodity is concerned with prestige, in that possession of foreign objects undeniably confers prestige. The ancient trade of the Pacific Ocean was prestige trade.

It was dangerous, often conducted across formidable distances. Established networks of trade existed, while the adventurous aimed to widen their trade contacts by opening new avenues off the usual networks. Active, virile communities traded more than others. Communities on the decline traded less.

Among the most important items in trade were new songs and dances. Prior to the departure of a trading expedition these, the latest and best, composed and devised on the atoll, would be rehearsed to perfection. Then a fine assortment of the atoll's most splendid mats, baskets and other manufactures would be put aboard, together with porpoise-tooth necklaces and other finery, fish-hooks – a Gilbertese fish-hook was a veritable work of art, besides being a foolproof contrivance – and money. Food for the journey would be laden. After the performance of magic ceremonies to ensure success, off they would go to their chosen destination, which might be more than a thousand miles away.

Navigation was the charge of certain men expertly trained to undertake long-distance voyages, their training including a seven-year course in astronomy.[1] The general run of atoll men were usually good voyagers in and around their home group. Long-distance voyages depended on trained experts.

After the tremendous ordeal of a voyage which might last several weeks, as they neared their destination they would usually sing one of their songs, a song at sea indicating a friendly visit. They would be welcomed ashore, and in due course there would be a grand reception for them in the *manéapa*, the huge meeting house which was the largest building in any community. At this reception, after lengthy speeches on both sides – interpreters accompanied long-distance voyages – the visitors would present their gifts to the entire community, amid multiple expressions of approval and admiration. Next day there would be a feast, after which the visitors would be invited to take the floor of the *manéapa* and 'teach the people some new songs and dances', i.e. perform. A day or two later there would be another feast, after which the hosts would show off their songs and dances to the visitors; and so on for several days of jollification.

Meanwhile the musicians on both sides settled down to some serious work learning each other's songs by heart. The words of these songs, relating to the latest religious ideas or accounts of daring exploits, were the Oceanic equivalent of up-to-date books, providing the means whereby the latest ideas spread with remarkable rapidity across great distances. Intellectually, the ancient Pacific was very wide awake.

On the eve of departure, the occasion of a huge feast, the return gifts would be presented, all of them local variants of the same commodities the visitors had brought, mats, baskets, shell money and so on. In all trade of this kind there were also specific items which were useful and otherwise unobtainable. Curiously enough, though, to exchange and obtain these was not the main object of the voyages.

If the visit had been a successful one, meaning that if there had been no murders, fighting or other unpleasantness, and if the visitors' gifts, after careful inspection, were deemed appropriate in

[1] For details, see Part IV, Chap. 9.

quality and quantity to the self-estimated dignity of the community visited, an endeavour would be made to ensure that, in quality and quantity, the return gifts were at least commensurate with those brought, erring on the side of exceeding them, and accompanied by a great deal of food for the return journey.

If the visit had been unusually successful, the return gifts might be more bulky and contain rare items, for each atoll had its valued antiques. Care had to be taken, however, not to give too much in such cases, since this might be construed by the visitors as an insult, an insinuation that their atoll must be rather a poor place. In any event, after a successful visit the voyagers could count on coming away with a little more than they brought, and could to this extent be said to have made a profit.

All required ceremonies having been performed, the traders would then set off on the long and perilous homeward voyage, bearing very slightly more of almost exactly the same things as they set out with. Innumerable expeditions doubtless foundered or were lost in the course of these extraordinary voyages. These were the risks men took.

Senseless, one would say today. Why did they bother to do it?

They did it for two related reasons, both of them fundamental to mankind. Firstly, man requires a challenge. Without one he becomes inert. Earlier on, it was explained how incentive, being peculiarly absent on an atoll, was artificially stimulated by means of magic. Challenge is similarly lacking, with the difference that man without a challenge will invent one, often quite improbable, even irrational.

The present century has witnessed the long and patient endeavours made by man to climb Mount Everest. What for? It is not as if one could live on it. Yet when Edmund Hillary and Tenzing reached the top and came down alive, mankind demonstrated its awareness of the deep human significance of challenge by giving them immediate universal acclaim. No one will deny that Oceanic man, in making his terrifying voyages, created for himself a momentous challenge.

The second reason for the voyages, part and parcel of the first, is that man likes to show other people what he can make and do. He has a basic need for the esteem of others. Esteem, however, operates on the same principle as profit. If it is not increasing, it is in reality diminishing; it cannot stand still.

On atolls, personal esteem, like nearly everything else, is static, thus diminishing. To satisfy man's need for the esteem of others, conditions had to be artificially created by voyages to faraway places, where after the tremendous hardships and difficulties of the voyage, the visitors basked in the esteem of others, inwardly reassuring themselves thereby, returning afterwards to enjoy the almost equal esteem of their own folk at beholding the massive trade outcome of the expedition, most of which was then *baboosed*.

These two profound human needs, the need for a challenge, and the need for the esteem of others, were the motives for what has come to be known as ceremonial trade, meaning that it was trade unconnected with profit.

This, the only kind of trade they knew, was what the atoll people brought into Insular Asia; and once again they encountered nothing that might have suggested converting it into something different.

The Melanesians, the principal people they encountered, had among their own islands and groups the same system of ceremonial trade – at any rate, apparently the same. Actually, in their own strange way, connected with the ascending grades in their society, many Melanesians understood the individual profit motive – it was connected with accumulating pigs and other valuables – and acted on this motive for reasons concerned with mounting the social hierarchy. In some places they even used manufactured shell money (their own) as an exchange item for obtaining valuable objects, among which pride of place was held by the pig – using money, in other words, as an item of barter.

Melanesian society was extremely diverse, however, and it may be that the generally superior atoll people did not encounter any of the groups who practised individual profit and used (among other things) money in a restricted sense.

Yet even where the atoll people did encounter such groups, there was an extra factor rendering it unlikely that they would ever have paid much attention to Melanesians, or learned from their more ancient (though in some ways more modern) approach to profit. The

Melanesians were black, and the brown-skinned atoll people found their girls unattractive. Bearing in mind the advanced knowledge and arts of the atoll people, this was not a situation which lent itself to their paying much attention to Melanesian ways, still less to learning from them.

The transferred atoll's assets and liabilities

From atoll strips, from specks in the ocean, they came to islands so large that it was impossible to tell by looking at them that they were islands. From an almost incredible deprivation imposed by nature – it is worthwhile recalling the ingredients of their diet: one tasteless root vegetable, tasteless fish, octopus and squid, a crab sometimes, a slightly salty coconut, a breadfruit sometimes, a small pandanus fruit and a dry and rather salty banana very occasionally – they came to the pullulating fertility of Insular Asia and, in Java, to the world's most fertile island, where almost anything will grow.

They brought with them their trade in which there is no profit. They brought their own special absence of profit motive or the individual urge to accumulate, accumulation being socially impossible on an atoll. They brought their own special concept of social balance, expressed in small communities geared to keep all members on the same level of wealth. They brought their money which was not used as a medium of exchange. They brought their custom of hard work unrelated to time or money – and of course with money entirely unrelated to time. They came with only rudimentary ideas of cooking.

And thus, with slight modifications, the great majority of them have remained ever since.

When, long after their settlement in Asia, they had their first encounters with continental civilization, most of the foregoing proved to be liabilities. Against these must be set their assets.

They brought their decorous, expressive languages, abounding in Oceanic imagery, and containing no swear-words.

They brought an advanced morality and law, usually referred to as custom, or in Indonesia, *adat*. Though law was unwritten, so deeply was *adat* ingrained that, even after handwriting was introduced from

3. Commemorating an ancient arrival – dragon boat racing in Hongkong.

No seasons – farmers harvesting rice in Indonesia; mid-distance, rice at half growth; far distance, young rice; foreground, land about to be used as a nursery.

4. The world's oldest parliament houses – a *maneapa* in the Gilbert Islands, the hall of assembly. Note the interior posts, each representing a clan. It was in buildings such as this that the student of long-distance navigation took his seven-year course in astronomy.

India, there was little need to write *adat* down, and this has widely remained so.

They brought a sophisticated system of community government, which fell into desuetude after the introduction of Hindu ideas of kingship.[1]

They brought their own religious ideas, which were universal in theme and ancestral in application. These were modified and nearly everywhere expunged as an outcome of direct contact with four of the world's major religions – Hinduism, Buddhism, Christianity and Islam.

They brought their own wholesome magic, which was similarly assaulted.

They brought an advanced art of vocal chorus music and dance, but no musical instruments, it being impossible to make any on an atoll.

With the later introduction of the buffalo and cow, whence gut for stringed instruments, and metal, whence the gongs of the *gamelan* (the Javanese percussion orchestra), and under the influence of Hindu dramatic art, music and the theatre developed and flourished in Java and Bali to become one of the artistic splendours of the modern world, though elsewhere it declined under various historical pressures.

They brought an unrivalled knowledge of navigation and an advanced knowledge of astronomy, which alike gradually declined over the centuries as a result of disuse.

They brought a number of interesting and sensible social customs aimed at keeping men calm and women cared for – such as that a man whose wife was with child might sleep with her unmarried younger sister, with the latter's consent, and if a married man died prematurely his younger brother could husband the widow. Most of these customs, of much value on an atoll, were practised widely in Insular Asia until suppressed by the continental religions.

Finally, in sharp contrast with most of Asia, they brought a society in which women were the equal of men in all respects, save that women did not have a public voice in government.

[1] See Part III, Chap. 7.

One of the reasons why there has been relatively so slight an adaptation to the broader conditions of a land area is to be sought in the atolls. The restrictions which an atoll imposes on man and society – the straitjacket conditions of man's life there – have had the effect that everything evolved there – thought, manners, pattern of society and life – being extremely restricted, is *concentrated*, rendering it unusually powerful and difficult to change.

PART III

The Transferred Atoll in Action

Quinquireme of Nineveh from distant Ophir
Rowing home to haven in sunny Palestine,
With a cargo of ivory
And apes and peacocks,
Sandalwood, cedarwood, and sweet white wine.

JOHN MASEFIELD: *Cargoes*

5 Austronesian Confines in Asia

The Oceanic mind in relation to continental land
When the atoll people came to Asia, they settled on coasts and in
estuaries. Being maritime, small-island people, they did not feel at
ease except near the sea. They had no desire to explore the interior,
regarding it as uninteresting if it was mountainous.

The degree of human conditioning which life on an atoll induces –
a *concentrated* conditioning – is remarkable in this respect.

On an atoll everything is dead flat, and one is everywhere conscious
of the ocean all around. The atoll is *part* of the ocean, a dry part.
Thus when going anywhere on foot, one does not go for a walk in
the way we do; one navigates. One does not go forwards, backwards,
right or left. One goes north, south, east or west. Asking someone
for directions, one will be told to go north, or go south, as the case
may be, then perhaps go west.

This is one of many features which have passed from the atolls
into Asia. In Java and Bali, asking for directions in Indonesian, even
in the middle of a town, these will be given with reference to north,
south, east and west, exactly as on an atoll. Ask for directions in
terms of right and left, and things end in a hopeless muddle. This is
not how people think who have a marine approach to land.

Moreover, first reactions of atoll people in contact with non-atoll
conditions are extraordinary. Some years ago, due to overpopulation
in the Gilberts, colonies of Gilbertese were settled in the Solomon
Islands – mountainous, forested and more bushy than a Gilbert
atoll.

The outcome was comic. Faced with pedestrian conditions in
which, at least on one side, there was definitely no ocean, and in
which one moment one was for some inexplicable reason going –
what was the word for it ? – up, while the next one was going – how to
describe the sensation ? – down, the land 'navigation' system broke

down. Ten minutes' walk from his settlement, a Gilbertese was utterly lost. It was a minor nightmare for those in charge trying to find them each evening and bring them home. Such is the extremity of atoll conditioning, induced by the limitations life imposes there, and to the fact that atolls belong to ocean rather than to land.

Among those who came to Asia were many from Pacific islands, as opposed to atolls. For them, familiar with mountains, there were less difficulties. All, however, shared the same sense of affinity to ocean, which in itself suffices to demonstrate the Austronesian attitude towards the interior of a country. It was not simply that they preferred to be near the sea. An interior was something entirely strange and foreign to them.

Nor were they lured by it. They felt no attraction for large blocks of land. The most striking example of this was the Gilbertese discovery of South America.

At some unknown time in the distant past, a Gilbertese fleet sailed on a voyage of discovery to the east. They sailed eastward for *four months*, till they sighted South America. Picturing a continental people in those vessels, it needs few words to describe the moment of excitement that first distant view of the Andes would have been, and the thrill of expectation as they neared the unknown coast.

This was not in the least how the Gilbertese, belonging to an Oceanic people, saw it. Though they were impressed, they saw South America not as a land of promise, but as an obstacle. They described it as Maiwa, 'the wall at the side of the world, four moons sail to eastward . . . a land that stretches to the north without end and to the south without end . . . beyond the furthest eastward island it lies – a wall of mountains up against the place where the sun rises'.[1]

They presumably landed for refreshments. If they did, this was all they did. Having seen the great wall of the Andes, they sailed back whence they came, another incredible four-month voyage, and recounted what they had found – which is how it is known today.

This reaction of an Oceanic people is the opposite to that of the Romans, a continental people, when, standing on the western shores

[1] Rosemary Grimble, *op. cit.*, p. 37.

of Iberia, they beheld the Atlantic and deemed it to be the end of the
world, an obstacle to further progress. To a continental people a
mass of ocean is classically an obstacle; to an Oceanic people a mass
of land is. This factor imposed its own limitations on the spread and
scope of the Austronesian world in Asia.

Coastal and riverine settlement—prestige and the spread of Oceanic languages

Austronesian inland penetration and settlement in Asia were by
river. Where there were no rivers, settlement remained coastal until,
in Java and Bali, rising population led to inward movement unrelated to large rivers.

Typical early centres of Austronesian settlement are, in Cambodia,
along the Mekong river leading into the Tonlé Sap, the great lake
lying just south of Angkor; and in the Philippines, along the Pasig
river leading from Manila Bay into Laguna de Bai, another inland
lake.

When they took to agriculture, hill rice was the first cereal
cultivated, though never far from the sea or a navigable river. The
later introduction of irrigation led many who had settled inland to
come down-river nearer to coasts, where on flat land they could
cultivate by moving about inland by boat, their natural form of
transport. This they were able to do in the low-lying rice-bearing
provinces of Luzon, along the flat, swampy eastern side of Sumatra,
and around the coasts of Borneo.

Though they eventually came to occupy fairly large parts of the
larger Philippine islands, Java and Bali are the only places where they
became fully land-based, and which they completely appropriated.
In Java, however, the conditions of being obliged to live in a land
mass were felt to be so strange that, everywhere they could, the
people unconsciously arranged themselves in a way which as closely
as possible re-created the conditions of their ancestral ocean.

When Europeans first came upon them, the Javanese were regarded as an agricultural people, which they had indeed become.
Yet the marine character of the civilization from which they were
descended remained with them in latent form. When the Dutch in

the eighteenth century, unable to obtain suitable local sailors to man their vessels, reluctantly concluded that there was no alternative to engaging Javanese, they were astounded by the natural way these 'agriculturalists' took to seaborne life, being specially impressed by their innate understanding of teamwork aboard ship, a faculty the Dutch found inexplicable.[1]

In some places, such as Celebes, the Austronesian attachment to the sea was such that they remained essentially coastal and seaborne, only taking to irrigation where swamp land made wet cultivation possible without the use of ingenuity or much effort.

As a result of this basic marine element in it, the depth of Austronesian influence and the atoll mentality today is more pronounced among coastal and lowland people than among those of the interior. Culturally, the inland and upland people lived on the fringe of the Austronesian world, though geographically the case could be stated in reverse. With the exception of Java and Bali, the Austronesians remained on the fringes of land.

Their indirect influence, however, extended beyond these fringes, notably in language. All the principal inland and upland people ended by speaking variants of Austronesian languages, to such an extent that their former pre-Austronesian languages were forgotten.

This at first suggests that the inland people were conquered and thrust back from coasts. In fact, the Pacific people came in peace. The great feature of this age was that it was a time of peace, a matter on which tradition is emphatic. A Melanesian tradition speaks of it as 'a Great Peace, when there was trade among all the islands, using large ships'.[2]

The remarkable linguistic outcome of this is sufficient to show that the Austronesians were everywhere seen as prestigious people, with whom it was an honour and an advantage to be culturally in contact. Where, as in Melanesia, there was ceremonial trade, such contacts fitted into an existing pattern. Elsewhere the contacts arose

[1] See Raffles' *History of Java*.

[2] This particular version of the tradition, one of the most specific, comes from San Cristóbal in the Solomon Islands, where it was related to Dr. Charles E. Fox, *infra*, Appendix 3.

from barter trade, rendered possible by the climatic condition that coast and upland differ in their natural products, and there is a reciprocal need for exchange. As an example, many upland areas are dependent on the coastal regions for salt, while the coasts depend on the interior for highly esteemed upland and jungle fruits, without which coastal diet is not properly balanced.

One of the reasons for the spread of Austronesian languages in Melanesia, which was a relatively highly populated region, was that nearly all groups warred with their neighbours. By enjoying good contacts with the peaceful but powerful and well-armed Austronesians, a declining group could gain prestige at the expense of hostile and stronger neighbours. For these and other strong motives of local advantage, the languages of a maritime people penetrated deeply into the interior of islands as large as Sumatra, Borneo and New Guinea, despite the Austronesians having no taste for interior travel.

This last, incidentally, remains a feature of the atoll-transferred people to this day, being particularly noticeable in jungle territories. An atoll-transferred man is reasonably at ease in the jungle as long as there is a navigable river. Beyond the point where the river ceases to be navigable he is more a handicap than a help. After a few days of the interior jungle he feels so completely miserable that he often ends by falling sick.

Apart from language, Austronesian influence was confined to what the people were mentally capable of taking in.

In the case of Melanesians, this was not much. Austronesian religious ideas, with their universal approach, had no effect on Melanesians whatever. Melanesian thought belongs to an age long before man in this part of the world had begun to think in terms of the universal, and the Austronesians' larger and newer ideas were more than Melanesians could take in.

For the same reasons, such knowledge of astronomy as the Pacific people were able to impart in Asia was only fragmentary. Most people found such matters beyond them, nor did astronomy have so wide an application to inland people as it had to a race of ocean travellers.

Basically, these were relations of prestige, a feature which becomes more understandable when one remembers that it was prestige which lay at the root of Oceanic ceremonial trade. Austronesian prestige accounts more than anything else for the fact that inland people in Melanesia and Insular Asia learned to speak – or more properly, drifted into speaking – Austronesian languages.

Inland people and Melanesia

The theory that inland people were thrust back to where they are today by pressure of more active and virile newcomers on their coasts, and withdrew inland with rudiments of newly acquired language, is not tenable in this region. It is possible that there were cases of withdrawal (though even then not from the coast) among some of the aborigines. There is, however, no evidence to support such a theory in respect of the more important tribal people, who live where they do, and seem always to have done so, for reasons of ingrained personal preference. A Land Dayak of Borneo shares with all the hill or 'bush' people of Melanesia a dislike of water which is not crystal clear from mountain streams. Visiting the coast, such people feel inwardly uncomfortable. They dislike having to wash in lowland well-water, however pure, and hate having to drink it. Nor is there anything in their traditions to suggest they once lived on the coast.

Moreover, the withdrawal theory suggests that inland people withdrew because they were the weaker of two in contest, which in this region is patently not so. In parts of the Solomon Islands, where 'bush' and coastal people lived in fairly close proximity, the coastal (saltwater) people were fierce enough, the 'bush' (freshwater) people fiercer still, so much so that coastal people were sometimes obliged to construct artificial islets on which to live offshore, setting water between them and the aggressive 'bush' people, who had no boats and could not swim.

A similar situation was found in Sumatra, where coastal people often lived in fear of the highland Batak people, who were superior to them, and in addition held the best terrain.

The most prominent and impressive of the inland people are in fact the Batak, who live in the uplands of north-western Sumatra, in fine, open countryside of steep hills and rolling upland plains, high amid which lies the scenically spectacular Lake Toba. The soil is not so fertile as in the lowlands, but the climate is invigorating and the scenery superb, providing an understandable instance of a people who live where they do because they prefer it.

Prior to their conversion to Christianity, the Batak were ritual cannibals. In other words, it would seem one was considering a people conspicuously more primitive than the surrounding lowland and coastal Austronesians.

With the deadening and inhibiting practice of cannibalism removed, the Batak, a land-based people with no atoll antecedents, have on the contrary shown themselves to possess many qualities which make them, in the Indonesian environment, singularly well-equipped to cope with conditions in the modern world of economics, amid which the greater number of all Indonesians with an atoll background are still where they originally were – at sea.

The Batak people always seem to have had a brisk barter trade among themselves, and with coastal people. When money first came, they quickly learned its uses. They became adept at mathematics to a rare degree in Insular Asia, and found no difficulty in relating money to time. This, combined with the Christian idea that what a man earns is his, has opened the door to thrift, individual and collective; and this thrift, or economic sense, is purposefully applied. When the Batak build stone houses facing a road, they build them in a connecting row, as Chinese do, to save time and money. The way they handle stone as a building material leaves much to be desired, but this is beside the point. The emergence of the Batak over the past hundred years has been little short of spectacular. In terms of personnel, the contribution they make to Indonesian public life far exceeds, in relation to size of population, that of any other ethnic group.

To the south-east of them, also in the Sumatra highlands, is the home of the Menangkábau, matriarchal and Muslim, and again without an atoll past, among whom some of the same characteristics are to be found. This general area of the Sumatra highlands is often referred to as the home of the best brains in Indonesia.

Elsewhere the inland people are less advanced than this. The Torája of Central Celebes are still fairly enclosed and remote, though their spectacular highlands provide another instance of a people who live where they do for preference, and whose inland and upland home is by far the best part of the island. The Dayaks of Borneo, living in a jungle region presenting great obstacles to movement, and with the difficult background of head-hunting in their past, have made what could be called a slower entry into modern life.[1]

Yet everywhere, among those who do not have the atoll background, the same tendencies are observable. The Dayaks have only been handling money for a few decades, yet Dayak commerce, particularly among the Iban of Sarawak, is now an established fact of life. This tendency of people formerly considered primitive to find their economic feet with greater ease than people hitherto considered civilized is one which is destined to continue.

The Melanesians, who are of course coastal as well as inland, have a built-in urge to personal accumulation, arising from the system of bride-prices. A Melanesian has to buy his wife, and bride-prices are in some places so high that one finds men of forty-five who have still not managed to save enough to get married.

The commodity in which the price is paid varies from place to place. In the Maumeré district of eastern Flores it is paid in horses – ten for an ordinary girl, more if beautiful or of high family. Further east, in the Larantuka region, it must be paid in antique elephant tusks imported from Portuguese Goa, whence export was discontinued around 1836.

The practice being for married women to make bangles out of their elephant tusks, the number of these in circulation lessens slightly each year, while the value of those that remain rises as their rarity increases. As can be appreciated, marriage in Larantuka is something of a nightmare.

On the island of Alor, still further east, the bride-price must be paid in the huge bronze drums known as *moko-moko*, dating from the fifteenth century – one *moko-moko* is the price of a bride.

[1] See Appendix 1: Perverse Cults.

This extraordinarily difficult and complicated system of getting a wife faces a Melanesian squarely with the importance of personal accumulation. On the rare occasions when one finds a Melanesian working on a salaried basis outside his homeland, he stands out from among his brown-skinned Indonesian colleagues by being the only one who is not in debt, his sense of accumulation having enabled him to see his salary in terms of time.

6 Commerce

The Austronesians, depending on what group of atolls or islands they came from in the Pacific, were as varied in temperament as are the people of the Pacific today. Some were stay-at-home, in the sense that, while prepared to undertake tremendous voyages at great personal risk in search of a better home, once they found somewhere better they made only local sea journeys. Others, on the other hand, were inveterate travellers and traders, their social life being purposeless without travel, their homes essentially places they left and returned to.

A combination of these two, the settlers and the travellers, set the tone in what followed the Austronesian arrival in Asia. Some, as in Java, settled and concentrated on local voyages. Others elsewhere settled but, like many tourists today, did not call a journey a journey unless it was international. These were the inveterate travellers whose activities in Asia are still discernible, and who unintentionally provided the *point d'appui* in continental man's discovery of the islands.

Continental man and insular man were unknown to each other.

The maritime discovery of the East
On entering Indonesian waters, the atoll people found themselves in a region where, with their knowledge of astronomy, it was remarkably easy to travel, once the pronounced seasonal changes in the prevailing winds were understood. They settled and explored.

Essentially drawn to islands – the only form of land with which they were familiar – in the course of their explorations they discovered Ceylon and Madagascar, on both of which small groups of them settled.[1] They discovered India. With such ease of communica-

[1] The classic approach of the Austronesians into Asia was determined by what is sometimes referred to as the 'outrigger route'. This runs from Tahiti, etc., westward

tions as exist in the Arabian Sea, they reached the Persian Gulf and the Red Sea.

Their contact there with Mediterranean civilization was obscure and tenuous, but it established a fragile bridge of communication. In some of the ancient religious stories of the Pacific there is a curious resemblance, in philosophic content, to some of the oldest Biblical stories, apparently stemming from this point of contact.

In East Asia they explored the South China Sea, and again settled on islands – the Philippines, Hainan and Taiwan. They reached Japan where, despite the rigours of winter, they settled, having a profound effect on language, ancestral ideas, and clan structure.[1] They are, in fact, the foundation element in present-day Japanese culture, their arrival establishing a connexion with lands to the south which was to endure for centuries, giving the Japanese – in all that relates to their non-Chinese past – their distinctive character of being part of a warm southern culture transposed to the cold north.

They visited and settled in estuaries in continental Asia. There, however, except in Cambodia, where the Khmer agriculturalists and the Cochin-Chinese (living largely in boats) bear many marks of the transferred atoll, their traces are indistinct. It would seem, however, that the southern part of the Indo-Chinese peninsula must once have ranked with Java and Bali as an area which the Pacific

---

across the equatorial Pacific, via the Coral Sea or (preferably) the northern coasts of New Guinea, the Indian Ocean south of Indonesia, thence north-west toward the Nicobars, thence south-west, passing south of Ceylon, and from there direct to the northern end of Madagascar. A well-provisioned small Pacific sailing ship of former times, with single outrigger – one of the fastest-moving vessels in the world – could make this immense journey with surprising ease. It was the existence of this 'natural' route for a swift vessel which caused Indonesia – and not the Philippines or Japan – to be the Austronesian discovery point in Asia, and base for further operations of discovery.

[1] Prominent among Pacific clans represented in East Asia were those of the Sun and the turtle. The clan of the Sun being the only one not having an ancestral animal, and the turtle being held in particular veneration, these two clans held a special position in the Austronesian world, being automatically senior to others. The Japanese Emperors, whose ancestor is of the Sun, would seem to be descended, in the manner explained here, from the senior Pacific clan.

people completely appropriated in respect of their culture and way of life, forming a southern and largely riverine *bloc* extending from the Mekong to the Irráwaddy, which they eventually bequeathed to their partial descendants, the Mon-Khmer.

Only on islands such as Taiwan and Hainan have they left direct descendants to make their presence known. Wherever, as on those two islands, one hears that distinctive vocal chorus music without any musical instruments to accompany it, it is a sign of being in the presence of Austronesia.

They were thus the first, so far as is known, to discover and exploit, in the interests of ceremonial trade, the modern shipping lines of the East. Due to the formal annual patterns of currents and monsoons, these routes have been regular, to within a hundred miles or so, since the beginning of international sea travel. Though to their discoverers they undoubtedly did not seem so, most of them are inevitable routes, dictated by wind and current.

None of the major civilizations of continental Asia had yet expanded to the coast – or, to be more specific in the case of the Indo-Chinese peninsula, the area of the Chinese culture had not expanded sufficiently to cause adjacent people (Burmese, Thai, Vietnamese) to be eased southward to reach a coast.

The coasts of India and China in those times were inhabited by people not dissimilar from Austronesians, inasmuch as they too were small group communities living beside and from the sea. They probably looked reasonably Indian and Chinese, though not yet Hindu or Chinese culturally. Their descendants can be seen to this day along the Coromandel coast, among the sub-caste and out-caste fishermen, who though transparently Indian, are distinctly un-Hindu in their thinking and ways. Others among them are racially different, and have red hair.

On the South China coast the people were red-skinned. Traces of them are still to be found, though they are rare. The survivors today are as Chinese as anyone else, save for the ruddy tint of their skin.[1]

To such people Austronesian ceremonial trade visits came as a

[1] Where I have come across these people, their mother-tongue proved invariably to be Hakka. Whether this has any significance is uncertain.

welcome excitement; and ceremonial trade, if it was not already known, fitted nicely into prevailing conditions, this being a tradeless region, none of the coasts having a commercial hinterland, acquisition of which would radically alter their character.

As in Oceania, so in Asia; different communities maintained contact with one another by means of ceremonial trade voyages. These, due to ease of travel and the predictableness of seasons, became regular. The seasons themselves – the two seasons of a northerly and a southerly wind – became part of the ceremonial.

In addition, where in the Pacific the amount of useful and otherwise unobtainable items in ceremonial trade constituted a minor feature, in Asia these rose to become the prime feature of trade, gradually altering it from ceremonial to barter trade. This feature of trade's usefulness, arising from long journeys between land areas rich in differing natural products, contributed to the regularity of such journeys.

In another way the voyages differed from those of the Pacific. Those made to the coastal people of continental Asia were not reciprocated by return voyages to the southern islands, the people not possessing ships which could match those of the Austronesians, nor their skill in navigation. By the coastal Asians these voyages were seen as annual events, when they were visited by people from the South.

Dragon boats

That these visits were a source of excitement, festivity and profit is shown in the several countries where they are still commemorated by annual boat races.

On the Menam in Thailand, on the Mekong river in Cambodia and Vietnam, in Hongkong and other places on the China coast, in Taiwan, and at Nagasaki in Japan, boat races – these days popularly called dragon boat races – are a feature of an important annual festival. This occurs at different seasons in the different countries, and in each country it has become identified with some person or event in that nation's history.

Each of these identifications is a contrivance, of which the Chinese version, relating the boat races to a poet who drowned in a lake, is the most contrived. By these contrivances a continental people sought to justify a 'barbarian' coastal festival.

When continental civilization at least reached out to the coasts of Asia, the first to arrive were individual pioneers.[1] Being few in number, they were obliged to conform to some extent in the matter of local customs and festivals, of which one of the most popular was that connected with the great event of the ancient year: the arrival of the trade boats from the South.

These trade voyages eventually ceased. On the last of them, a few men and boats inevitably remained behind, and these boats were taken out once a year, at the appropriate arrival time, and manned partly for old time's sake, and partly, in the early years, as a magical inducement to cause another fleet of ceremonial traders to come. None did, but these annual outings of the old trade boats became a festival.

When, long after the continental pioneers arrived, continental officialdom followed, the mandarins and others found to their disdain that their own people were taking part in the barbarian boat festival which, too popular to be suppressed, had somehow to be accommodated and made respectable. This was done by associating it with some famous person or event from the continental background of the new arrivals. Such frauds were simple to perpetrate. They were in writing, and the coastal people could not read.

A dragon boat, to take an example from Hongkong and the Pearl River, is a long and sturdy plank-constructed canoe, manned by between forty and sixty paddlers, with a helmsman aft, and amidships a large drum, with a drummer to give the pace of the stroke.

This is a typical Austronesian vessel, a ceremonial model of its larger trading prototype. The Gilbertese favoured sailing craft, but many other Pacific people travelled in large paddled canoes. In their classic form these had an outrigger. In Asia, with better timber and

[1] This fact is amply borne out in examining the foundation stories of Chinese coastal villages. In each case 'foundation' started with the arrival of one – sometimes two – Chinese from further inland, who settled among coastal people who eventually became Chinese. See also Appendix 5.

stone implements instead of coral, it became possible to dispense with the outrigger, which was thereafter only used for slender lake and coastal craft.[1] With long-journey vessels, if a sail was used, it was adjunct to the main means of locomotion, which was the paddle.

The drum would have been introduced after the buffalo and the cow were brought to Indonesia from India, when it became possible to make drums. In earlier times the pace of the paddle stroke was set by singing rhythmic songs, as was still the custom with the *barangay*, the Philippine version of this same craft, when the Spaniards first came.[2]

Thanks to archaeological studies made on islands in the Hongkong region, and to the strong continuity of tradition among the Cantonese, this is an area in which a particularly clear impression of ceremonial trade can be obtained.

In China the Dragon Boat Festival takes place on the fifth day of the fifth moon, usually in early May, when the south-east monsoon has just set in, and the summer rains start. This date marks to within a few days the regular arrival time for ceremonial trade voyages to China, travelling with the wind, and avoiding the sharp Chinese winter; the vessels returning south in the autumn, at the end of the south-east monsoon. A feature of Chinese dragon boat races is that when they are held on a seashore and in a traditional manner, the boats race from a point out at sea, straight into shore, signifying (though this is no longer remembered) the commemoration of an *arrival*.

The excavations on Lantao and Lamma, both of them islands in the group at the mouth of the Pearl River, reveal evidence of considerable human activity, including the slaughter of animals for meat, though with no permanent structures. These were temporary settlements, erected each year to accommodate the ceremonial traders and those who came from the interior to welcome them. The

[1] Another reason for dispensing with the outrigger was that these vessels carried cargo (amidships) and were thus heavily weighted, a factor which lessens the usefulness of an outrigger.

[2] See Antonio de Morga: *Sucesos de las Islas Filipinas*.

buildings were of matshed, a form of construction still widely used, which reached China in this way from Indonesia.

The Pearl River in those times was infested with crocodiles.[1] Rather than risk their visitors entering the river and running into difficulties, the local people, in their own river craft, came down annually to rivermouth islands such as Lantao and Lamma, in open sea well away from crocodiles, where they built new matshed residences and made other preparations in expectation of the traders' arrival. This, as is shown by the manner in which the dragon boat races are conducted, was one of the great moments of their year.

No one lived permanently in the area. When all was over, the islanders paddled home south, while the local people returned past the crocodiles to their homes further inland, leaving the matsheds to fall to pieces and rot.

This is an example of what was happening in many parts of Asia during the Austronesian period.

It is also exemplary of the fact that in this period it is useless to look for cities. There were none.

The meeting of continental and insular man

The major civilizations of Asia, such as they were at this time, were land-based to a pronounced degree, their societies agrarian, their kingdoms military. To them, as to the Romans, an ocean meant the end of the world. None of the rulers and men of affairs had seen the sea; many may not even have known of its existence.

It is not known where these two disparate brands of civilization – continental and Oceanic – first met, nor when. From an examination of the historically known consequences of those first meetings, each of which had certain features in common, it can, despite such a disadvantage, be perceived what happened on such occasions.

The simplest method of explaining this – it was a standard development with only minor variants – will be to tell an imaginary story, shaped as closely as it can be made to the probable.

[1] The famous story of Han Yu, the great essayist and administrator, ridding South Chinese rivers of crocodiles indicates that some of these were still crocodile-infested as recently as the ninth century A.D.

The meeting of continental and Oceanic civilization was an encounter of radically different minds. It was in this sense a dramatic situation, best explained by trying to re-create the moment.

Thus:

On the unpromising and largely barren shore of the island of Qeshm, at the mouth of the Persian Gulf, there lived an uninspiring community of proto-Arabs, one of several, living by fishing, with some small barter trade. They had occasional contacts with Aryans, an emerging people from the mainland. One or two of the proto-Arabs could speak some Aryan words.

From time to time along these shores came long paddled boats manned by lively, brown-skinned men wearing few clothes. They traded such goods as they had – nothing of much interest – but were difficult when it came to handling the tokens which (a recent innovation from the mainland) were now being used as money. Instead of accepting a proper amount of these tokens, they wanted them all.

One day a mainlander came to Qeshm with a man he said was his brother. They were possibly Aryans, or perhaps even Hittites. Whoever they were, they were throw-outs on their beam ends, as were all mainlanders who strayed so far from society and authority as to reach a coast.

These two were itinerant petty traders. They had some goods with them. The Qeshm people, though, in addition to living at the end of the world, were a mean bunch from whom there was nothing much to be gained. Only desperation had brought the two men there.

It so chanced that their visit coincided with the arrival of two boat-loads of Austronesians – cheerful, half-naked ruffians who the Qeshm people said were great thieves. Qeshm itself being known as a den of thieves, this was not a compliment. However, desperation dictating, the mainland trader sent the 'brother' to investigate. He returned saying it was impossible to trade with these people; they simply snatched everything they saw.

The trader was not put off by this talk of thieving. In his own way, he was a thief himself. Leaving the brother with the merchandise, he went to the beach. There he found that these unknown people, though light of limb, were tough and daring in nature, and engaging. They had a language, too, which was surprisingly easy to pick up. After a few days of meeting them ashore, the trader found himself using a number of their words.

It appeared that these men came from islands which were green – in Qeshm this symbolized the paradisal – where life was easy, with little need for work. In one of those split-second decisions which so often alter the course of events, the trader asked if they would take him with them when they set off. To his amazement, they agreed. Only a desperate man would have dared take such a venture into the unknown.

After four or five days at sea, the two men found they could converse a little in the new language. Their main worry was their merchandise, which had to be protected day and night from being pillaged and shared out.

Despite being a throw-out, the trader had intelligence. He quickly saw that these people had a different idea of property; everything in the boat in some way belonged to everyone. To put a stop to the day-and-night vigil, in which the two men were obliged to take it in turns to sleep, he tried to explain to them that he could not share out the goods, because these were being brought for their king.

Nothing he could say could get this idea across. It seemed they had no king, not even a chief. When he inquired about there being one man with power among them, they did not understand what he meant.

'But there are men above you,' he managed to say.

After endless misunderstanding they caught it. Yes, they replied, there were the 'old men'.

This, though the trader did not know it, meant either the ancestors or the elders. It sounding suitable enough, he explained that the merchandise was for the 'old men'. This received immediate acceptance, there being no more attempts to pilfer.

On the way, they called in at various places on the Malabar coast, as well as in Ceylon, where the crew had numerous friends speaking another language which they could understand with ease.

On the next section of the voyage, lasting a month, between Ceylon and Sumatra, the two continentals nearly died of thirst, until they forced themselves to do as the others did, drinking coconut water, and such rainwater as they were lucky enough to collect, mixed with sea-water and fish blood.[1] They were a nuisance to the others because they took more than their fair share of coconuts. But they survived. By the time they all reached the south-eastern coast of Sumatra, after several more weeks at sea, amicable conditions prevailed, and the traders felt entirely at ease with the language.

They arrived at a large wooden settlement situated beside a river, the houses built on stilts, some of them over the water. Here they were welcomed by the elders, among whom there was one who seemed to be senior. To him they addressed themselves particularly.

In the transferred atoll it was assumed that the pioneers had come – albeit in a strange way, not in their own boat – for prestige reasons, all travel being for such purposes fundamentally. When, at a meeting of the community, the trader proffered as imposing a selection of his merchandise as he could muster, this was considered to be a cere-monial presentation, provoking the usual expressions of commenda-tion. His explanations about the worth and value of the merchandise gave gratification.

But when, at the end of the meeting, after girls had taken the presentation away, the trader demanded money, this was considered bad manners. Money there was, and he would certainly be given some, along with equally desirable things, when the time came to leave. But to want money and nothing else, and to ask for it at once, was immodest, the kind of behaviour which demands a gentle reprimand.

The trader's hot reaction to this was the nearest point the situation came to disaster. He was mollified, however, by assurances on all sides that he had nothing to worry about; he would in due course be given money.

Meanwhile, having to wait till the monsoon changed, he cast about for local products to buy with the money (tokens) of his own

[1] In addition, after a heavy equatorial shower the skimmed water surface of the sea is fresh enough to drink.

he had brought, the value of which he would have to explain to these people, once he knew the value of their money. He settled mainly for curiosities, oddments to tickle a lady's fancy, the bones or teeth of unknown animals which some charlatan back home could pretend was medicine, and so on. Serious trade often starts from frivolous beginnings. When, after first encounters, steadier trade set in, scented woods and gum were among the earliest commodities.

He soon realized that it was useless to proffer money, either theirs or his, for what he wished to obtain. This kind of transaction was not understood. What he wanted could be assembled against the time of his departure, however, which seemed reasonably satisfactory.

After some weeks he discovered that the region was a source of benzoin, a valuable resin which he saw at once he could sell in quantity in his own country. It took time to collect, and he only managed to obtain a little before it was time to leave.

Having by now become friendly with the senior elder, he explained to him the importance of money in lands far away, saying that if the elder could arrange for a goodly supply of benzoin, he would return next year to fetch it, and that by developing a regular trade the elder could make a great deal of money.

This was understood. Money had always been highly esteemed. The more a community had of it the better.

When the monsoon changed, and the two men returned on the first ceremonial trade voyage of the new season – they were really barter voyages by this time – he had done a reasonable trade, and had the elder's assurance that a goodly supply of benzoin would be ready for him next year.

After another thirst-ridden crossing of the Bay of Bengal, the traders returned safely to their country, where they made their way to the nearest centre of habitation.

Production of the benzoin samples altered their situation overnight. A group of merchants combined with them to raise the capital required to make the next voyage, this time in their own ship, amply provided with earthenware jars for water. Two journeys in an Austronesian vessel sufficed for a lifetime.

The trader had taken a careful note of the route and seasons to be followed. He had also taken the precaution of asking two of the Sumatrans to stay behind to act as pilots and interpreters.

Next year, or the year after, they duly returned to Sumatra, where they were welcomed, their ship causing much interest. But they found that nothing had been done to collect benzoin. They had to start from the beginning again. Their ship being slower than an Austronesian canoe, only a small quantity of benzoin could be assembled before the monsoon changed, and they would have to be off. They ran the risk of a loss.

The truth was, of course, that, work being unconnected with time, none was done till there was a necessity for it, i.e. till the traders returned, which from their point of view was when it was too late.

Knowing that he was on to a good thing, the trader was vexed. He was privately furious. But he was quickly learning. He realized that these were people who, while knowing all there was to know about seasons, had no idea of ordinary time. He therefore did what trade he could, repeated his order for benzoin, and *left a man behind*.

Insular Asia's first expatriates

Whether the first trader originally came in an Austronesian vessel, or whether he came in his own, navigated by an Austronesian, and from whichever country he came, the foregoing are the basic ingredients of the situation which arose from the first meeting of ceremonial trade with trade for profit – an intermediary coastal people with inland as well as maritime contacts; an easy language which encouraged the venturesome to sail forth in the certainty of being understood; a series of misunderstandings to begin with; the discovery of a commodity of value; the rapid transposition to continental vessels, slower but better provided than the longboats; and in every case, and whatever the exact circumstances of it, wherever profitable trade could be engaged in, sooner or later *a man had to be left behind*.

Had these been barbaric people, the outcome would have been different. But they were not barbaric. Though simple by continental standards, they were in some ways highly civilized.

Assuming that the first trader came from the Middle East, it may be worth mentioning that the Chinese encountered precisely the same problem wherever they went – in the Philippines, Borneo, Timor and elsewhere – and solved it in the same way, except that, for security's sake, they would usually leave four or five men, rather than one.

Chinese seasonal trade with Insular Asia is getting on for three thousand years old. When this early trade is called seasonal, it does not mean that all the Chinese came and went each season. As the junks of the new season sailed into their familiar anchorages, ashore in every place were four or five Chinese to meet them.

The formation of a commercial society

So, to continue the story, what happened to the man who was left behind?

His first off-season on his own was the most difficult. Somehow he had to evolve inducements to persuade people to collect benzoin *before* the trader returned, so that by the time he sailed again there would be enough with which to set a profitable trade. One way he could have done this was to be unusually active in food-gathering, thereby enabling him to make presents of food to individuals who would otherwise have had to gather it themselves.

The next off-season his situation became easier. Having now learned that trade items were regarded as gifts, the trader on his third visit made the conventional ceremonial presentation to the elders, but was careful to keep the bulk of his merchandise in reserve, with the result that the man left behind now had a shop.

Trade being frivolous to start with, the shop dealt in little other than curiosities. But these pretty and amusing things could only be obtained by proferring money or benzoin. One way or the other, by paying men or bartering with them for benzoin, the resident trader was in a position to get work done.

Not regular work, of course; that was out of the question, due to the demands of fishing, hunting and hill rice cultivation. What he could obtain was work when there was a necessity for it, i.e. when a man or woman wanted to buy something from him. Slowly the community moved on to a form of money economy, in which money became related to work, though not to time.

Meanwhile, as the trader had said it would, the community was amassing money, vastly outranking its neighbours in prestige. The 'new' use of money in trade being integral to this auspicious rise in prestige, it was obvious that the community's money had to be looked after with care. It can be taken as certain that the trader's representative, in his own interests as well as in those of the community (the two were now identified, and he had married a ravishing beauty), advised that the special task of looking after community money be entrusted to one man.

The senior elder, considering himself too old for so onerous a duty, opted out. One of the younger elders was chosen. Whoever he was, as the guardian of public money he imperceptibly developed from an elder into a chief – a feature new to the community.

Inevitably, this nascent chief stood in urgent need of advice from the only man who understood money in its new trading sense. The resident trader became the community's financial adviser, responsible to the chief. This pattern – the chief and his foreign financial adviser and organizer – was to be perpetuated.

Not only had the community money by this time become important, it had been concentrated in one place, in a treasury, which had to be guarded from members of the community who, knowing it to be community money, could see no reason why it should not be given to them when they wanted some. Also, the community's exceptional prestige was arousing the jealousy of neighbours. Special men were required to guard the treasury.

Hitherto, every man had been an all-purpose man, each able to put his hand to more or less anything, including defence. There was now a modification to this. Soldiers came into being.

Only a few at first. However few, they presented the problem that they were non-productive. They had to be fed, and occasionally given some money when they did well. Above all, fed. The chief, too, as guardian of public money, had become non-productive; he too needed to be fed.

Feeding the non-productive concerned rice. Obtaining fish, fruits, and such vegetables as seeded themselves presented few problems, every man being a landowner (or a slave). A division had to be made in the hill rice grown by the community as a whole, setting aside from each person's share of the group crop a certain amount for the feeding of the chief and those who worked for him on a full-time basis.

A small new group of men came into being, skilled at measuring crops, judging as to quality, arranging for transport, and generally exercising control over others. As communities and territories expanded, these men assumed charge of individual lands, becoming as it were land sub-chiefs, they too and their men being fed from the community crop. Each became an administrative landlord, developing special abilities often bequeathed to the next generation, causing to come into existence a small hereditary class of men of responsibility and general ability, rooted in land and the measuring of rice. All of them were in addition members of the upper of the two castes into which society was divided, as will be explained in a later chapter.

It is noticeable in the Philippines today how nearly all the larger indigenous enterprises are controlled by people from landowning families; and the same feature is exhibited in the public life of Indonesia, Malaysia and Ceylon, in which men and women with a landed background play an unusually prominent part in affairs.

The origin of this is as described above. Most of them are descendants of that group which came into existence as an outcome of the atoll-transferred society's encounter with trade for profit.

Though not conspicuous in their ability to handle money (handling money in relation to time was not required of this group), they display qualities in administering, decision-making, and judgment (measuring and assessing quality) which set them to this day as a group apart and superior, their inheritance of experience being different from that of the great majority of their countrymen.

In Ceylon, where an Austronesian group was established alongside the native Vedda people and others, with a slight but steady influx of Indian men, marrying Austronesian girls and forming a mixed race of Indian appearance and Pacific temperament, the rice-measuring group dominated society, as it has ever since. Despite later heavy Indian immigration in the sixth century B.C., and the departure of many Austronesians for Madagascar, this element in the social pattern remained unchanged. Every Singhalese of real prominence during the colonial period was a descendant of this upper class of rice-measurers, as has been every prime minister of Ceylon since independence.

Thus came the first breaks with the society of the all-purpose man, which is pre-eminently the society of atolls, and still is. These breaks came as a result of continental contact, the all-purpose man having by that time ceased to be a feature of continental life.

Time and money

In respect of the time–money relationship, what effects did these new divisions of occupation have?

The chief, responsible for public money, had to know something about it. He had to face the fact, impressed upon him by his foreign adviser, that part of the money had to be set aside for commercial purposes, on which the community's enhanced prestige depended. The rest the chief could spend in such measure as suited him and the community in general. Thus the chief had a large sum of money at his disposal which he could handle without relation to time. He at least learned to be careful, however, in terms of bulk. By looking into the treasury he could *see* when he was running low.

The rice-measurers, of the same social rank as the chief, did not have to handle money except for their own private use, thus remaining unaware of the importance of the time–money relationship.

The soldiers received their rice after harvest, together with (occasionally) money for personal use, which they spent without reference to time, thereby not learning the secret.

No one else learned it either. All in their small ways used money, and money was related to work – meaning work when there was a necessity for it, such as a desire to buy something. Money was not related to time, however. Not being so related, it circulated within the community impotently.

A society was thus formed in which the chief had become a trader – his community's *sole* trader – with a vague grasp of money. Only one man had to handle money in relation to work and time – the foreign financial adviser. The rest used money, but remained unaffected by it.

Chiefs in some places became kings, and kingdoms occasionally expanded into empires. This commercial pattern remained the same in all its essentials.

Here ends the imaginary – though maybe not so imaginary – story.

The Sri Vijaya empire

Dimly discernible in history, there were commercial empires in Indonesia under indigenous rule, a development which at first sounds improbable in terms of the transferred atoll.

The most famous of these empires, and the earliest, is Sri Vijaya, the Sacred and Victorious, a commercial empire with a dynasty of indigenous Hindu maharajas, who held sway between the seventh and twelfth centuries A.D. From its capital at Palémbang, in south-eastern Sumatra, this empire controlled much of Sumatra and West Java; the Malay peninsula as far north as the isthmus of Kra, in modern Thailand; and the commercially vital Strait of Malacca.

This and other later empires functioned on the same principle of treasurer-chief and foreign financial adviser, being large-scale versions of the same pattern, the king being the sole trader, the rest of the people having nothing to do with international commerce.

The connexion between treasury and chief was physical. The first treasury was in or part of the chief's house. With the coming of Hinduism, and the development of the idea of kingship, though this connexion between treasury and ruler remained the same, it acquired cosmic overtones.

Ceremonies had to be performed at the king's enthronement whereby he became imbued with attributes of deity, of which he was an emanation. The treasury, formerly the symbol of prestige, became the physical proof of the validity of the king as a divine emanation. The greater the amount of wealth in the treasury, the more absolute the king's divinity.

The treasury was situated in the royal compound. When enthroned, the king sat immediately in front of the treasury, with its doors behind him.

However large the empire or kingdom, the royal and divine ruler remained its sole trader.

In the case of a large and prosperous empire such as Sri Vijaya, the number of foreign personnel – mainly Indian – enlarged. Where there had been one foreign financial adviser, here there were several. In addition, foreigners managed any government office handling money. The king, as ever, did nothing with money, except dole it out and *watch* it.

Sri Vijaya's commercial importance depended on its control of the Strait of Malacca, the vital sea artery through which ran a developed continental trade between the Middle East, India and China.

The Strait of Malacca was patrolled in an irregular way (men went to sea when there was a *necessity* for it, not on any regular basis) by fleets or squadrons of small, swift vessels, manned by armed men who were ferocious fighters, their duty being to waylay every passing ship and 'invite' it into a Sri Vijaya port. Any who refused such an invitation were liable to be slaughtered to the last man, their ship with all its cargo being then towed into port as prize.

These activities have been called piratical. In reality they were not. The murderous squadrons were a local equivalent of customs and revenue vessels; and these were territorial waters, the king controlling *both* sides of the strait.

It is the squadron crews and their commanders who are of particular interest, however. These were men who presumably had to be fed (rice) and paid. How was this done?

Each commander, who was of relatively high birth, in a sense owned his men, to the latter's advantage. Men in such groups vied with one another over the eminence of their particular commander. The more eminent the leader (enjoying perhaps the king's favour), the more enviable was it to be one of his men. They did not exactly serve their leader, nor were they paid. They were simply his group, sharing their fortunes with him as 'his' men, enjoying a life that was the more esteemed as it was devoid of responsibility.

Occasionally a commander might be on the royal pay-roll for rice, in virtue of relationship or rank. Otherwise he, like 'his' men, would have land of his own, to which he might be obliged to return at sowing and harvesting, the land being otherwise looked after by family members or slaves. Being all of them part-resident in the royal city, however, they were more dependent than most on money.

When, having brought a ship into port, two or three commanders, themselves temporarily penniless – this was why they went to sea – presented themselves to the king and reported their success, he, having received professional (foreign) advice on the approximate value of the trade to be expected, rewarded his commanders by making each a gift from the treasury.

There was little or no system about it. The gifts were not weighed, for example. Consisting of currency of different lands, trinkets, odd bits of jewellery and other valuables, they would simply be handed to the commander in what looked like a suitable amount for him to get on with.

And there was sense in this. Weighing scales would have led to dangerous rivalries, whereas on the king's whim all could equally congratulate themselves. The king simply had to be careful. Apart from this, where money was concerned he led a very easy life.

The commanders would then withdraw, to find 'their' men waiting for them at the gates. Men of eminence in this part of the world invariably moved about with 'their' men in droves.

In their different droves they would go off for a feast, or to whatever else amused them. The money and valuables were distributed according to no particular principle. Someone might fancy an earring, and be given it. Another might ask for the small golden betel-set which was part of what the king had given. Such items could be enjoyed while the going was good, sold when necessary.

Money reached the individual hand in the same way, as seemed appropriate to the moment, with no idea of relative values, the money being in chips and nuggets of different shapes and sizes, and of various metals. What was valuable was not so much the money as the excitement of buying things with it, in which an astute buyer might obtain much more for far less than the next man. Where there is no urge to personal accumulation, considerations of having been given a dollar less than the next man count for little that can cause trouble. Next time, after all, it may be the other way round. So what?

Thus the transferred atoll moved towards modern times, scarcely changing.

Malacca in the fifteenth century

In the fifteenth century, in Malacca, it moved into the fringe of history, where, reconstructed from the pages of Tomé Pires' *Suma Oriental*, it can be seen indirectly – essentially the same.

The foreign financial advisers were by this time Indian Muslims from Gujerat, with a few from Tamil Nad. The wealth and commercial importance of Malacca – it was one of the richest cities in the world – necessitated a fair-sized bureaucracy, and, if Malacca's status was to be maintained, an efficient one. Every department handling money, even though it may have been headed by someone indigenous, was in fact controlled by an Indian subordinate responsible to him, following the pattern of the original foreign financial adviser, subordinate to the chief.

As ever, the king, or sultan, was the city's sole trader. As ever, all the public services were provided with rice. There were no salaries.

If a departmental head distinguished himself, the sultan would bestow a bounty on him from the treasury. This, under Islam, had become more modern, less cosmic than under Hinduism.

Apart from this, the functionaries lived on perquisites which became standardized, derived from tonnage dues, specific items of import and export, ship repair fees, and smaller items such as fees on the number of crew carried in foreign vessels, and on the number allowed ashore. Part of these fees went to the treasury, part were by custom purloined by the department concerned.

Within a department there existed a civil version of the commander and 'his' men. Departmental subordinates stood in a similar relation to their lord, or office head, with the result that when there was perquisite money to be had, everyone benefited in one way or another, while supplementary perquisites could be made individually by importuning foreigners ashore, and so on.

The atoll system of every man being a landowner persisted. Virtually everyone had his modest plot of coconuts, fruit trees and such vegetables as seeded themselves. The pettiest functionary, given free rice, could if necessary live without money.

This in turn produced a condition in which money, when available, was spent on finery rather than food, unless it was food for a wedding or some other ostentation. The intrusion of money produced a people who dressed well, but ate poorly; and this has continued to this day everywhere in the Malay-Indonesian world. An obstacle to the transferred atoll making adaptations is that the people's starting-point is one of centuries of inadequate diet, caused by the curious way in which money as an exchange medium entered their society.

The wealth of Malacca was evident to the eye, in the distinction of people's wearing apparel and the civilized comfort of their ornately carved wooden homes. There was obviously money in the place. Among the indigenous majority it was spent without regard to accumulation.

The senior dignitaries, all from that upper group associated with land supervision and rice measurement, lived in a stately style that matched the respect they received for their judgment and opinions. Many had sources of wealth aside from their official or semi-official perquisites. Some owned rentable ricefields in the country, or valuable orchards. All had 'their' men. In their way they were men of substance. In public affairs they were definitely so, owing to the influence they wielded.

Yet attempt to raise from any of them a sum of money for an enterprise in the merits of which they concurred, and it would be found that, in cash terms, they were little better off than the rest. Only a fraction of what was needed would be raised.

For money on this scale, it was necessary to turn to an Indian. The resident Indians, whether functionary or trader, were the intermediaries between state trade and international traders, and were the only ones who were men of economic and financial substance. Apart from them, only the sultan possessed real wealth, and he only thanks to Indian advice and care.

Malacca was like every other atoll-transferred city. Men of financial substance, being rare and ethnically alien, were constantly subject to gentle importunity. For a senior dignitary to beg a loan would be undignified, though doubtless it often happened. A more decorous method of procedure was to impose an additional 'duty' on someone's merchandise, or find some default in procedure which could be 'permitted' to pass 'unnoticed' if a gift was made to 'someone'.

Where money was concerned, everything for the indigenous depended on the next ship. Thus importunity became particularly irksome at times when, for a week or so, no ship arrived. At such times, though there would be no outward sign of it, the indigenous, high and low, were running low in cash. Perquisites being their sole avenue to cash, these were supplemented, in the manner described, by unofficial taxes and bribes.

To an alien this was not without its advantages. To have in fee a senior dignitary, possibly having intimate access to the sultan, could prove useful on occasion. Among the adept, this choice balance of interests led to many a senior dignitary being invisibly propped up financially, as a long-term insurance policy.

Had the functionaries been given salaries, it would alas! have made no difference. Two weeks with no ship, and everyone would be temporarily broke just the same. In fact, when a foreign vessel arrived after such a lull, one of the features that gave rise to complaint among visitors was that, in addition to paying heavy dues, they found themselves, all along the line, tipping people great and small. These tips were the functionaries' 'salaries'.

Indonesia—Portuguese, Dutch and Republican

In the sixteenth century the Portuguese reached the great goal of their voyages, the Spice Islands. Here they found two adjacent but rival empires, Ternaté and Tidor – two small, adjacent volcanic islands, each controlling a diversely scattered empire of spice-bearing islands, the ensemble having the effect of a chessboard from which all the pieces have been removed save for the two kings, who are side by side.

Each of these small islands had the same atoll-transferred pattern of commercial management. The foreign financial advisers here were Muslims who either fled or were disposed of by the Portuguese, at that date strongly anti-Muslim. In both Ternaté and Tidor, trade in spices could be conducted only through the sultan, government operating on the basis of the sultan's fabulous wealth, from which he distributed largesse.

Developments followed on classic lines, a resident Portuguese imperceptibly becoming the sultan's financial adviser. The same happened in Macassar, and in smaller kingdoms on Flores and elsewhere.

These latter-day events, being clear in history, reveal an aspect of this classic situation which would otherwise be uncertain. Despite his peculiar dependence on him, the king did not resent his foreign adviser. On the contrary, he esteemed him, in that by securing and increasing the king's wealth he was assuring the state's prestige. The esteem in which the Portuguese advisers were held was such that in every instance the ruler, no matter how wealthy or powerful, ended by speaking fluent Portuguese, being pleased to refer to the king of Portugal as his liegelord.

In 1641, after the fall of Portuguese Malacca to the Dutch, the Sultan of Macassar, one such Portuguese-speaking sovereign, welcomed refugeee Portuguese Christians from Malacca, permitting them to settle in his territory. The historic antipathy between Christian and Muslim had ceased to be of account.

A similar relationship of esteem without resentment evidently characterized this classic situation from its prehistoric beginnings, wherever the foreign adviser had the wisdom to behave with decorum.

When the Dutch extended their sway in Java, they did so by indirect rule, using the existing machinery of government, in which the key factor was the small group with inherited experience relating to land and rice measurement. Thereby this group reached the present age without being unduly interfered with. As might be expected, their descendants today provide the backbone of Indonesia's civil and military administration.

All that happened in Java under the Dutch was that money became more of a factor in relation to crops, while in each territorial area the senior administrator found himself with a Dutch superior.

During Dutch times, in fact, the main features of the transferred atoll as a commercial concern continued unaltered. The treasurer-chief, who had become a treasurer-king, was replaced under the Dutch by a treasurer-organization, the Netherlands East India Company.

As with the former kings, this combined the functions of government, treasurer, and monopoly trader, sole beneficiary of international trade, from the profits of which largesse was distributed in the form of public works and administrative salaries.

The mass of the Indonesian people continued, as before, to have no responsibilities in respect of international commerce, on which the state was dependent for its existence.

Landed gentry continued, as before, to collect rice and other crops, measuring the government's share of these.

The only persons of financial substance continued, as before, to be resident aliens – Chinese – who were in the usual intermediary position, though less subject to importunity.

Among 99% of the population money continued, as before, to circulate impotently.

With the transposition from colonialism to independence, the place of the Netherlands East India Company (the place of the treasurer-trader-king), which had been superseded by colonial administration, has been taken by a republican government. This has either a monopoly control or the major interest in every important exploitable commodity. The government is, as the kings were, the only entity of real wealth in the entire country.

As ever, it is assisted and run by men of experience and ability, with only a hazy idea of money.

As ever, it is dependent on the advice and organization of the non-indigenous and foreigners (many of these now organizations, not individuals) for obtaining local items of trade, a process known these days as 'the development of resources'.

As ever, the only elements of financial substance, apart from the government, are the resident non-indigenous, standing in a position of intermediary between the state's trade and other interests.

As ever, no one apart from them handles money purposively.

Functionaries, civil and military, are no longer paid in rice – though the police still partly are. Instead, they are paid salaries which, because few of the recipients understand the practical application of the relationship between money and time, have aggravated the perennial problem of importunity. Never has resort been made on such a scale to the system whereby functionaries in senior positions are invisibly propped up by the wealthy in search of advantage and gain.

As in fifteenth-century Malacca, unofficial 'taxes' and bribes, paid by the non-indigenous, provide a main source of cash for many a senior functionary's maintenance of status, the cash being spent, as usual, more on finery than food, the finery these days featuring cars and jewellery.

Contemporary Jakarta, a city of some 6,000,000, is in fact a large-scale version of the social and commercial pattern which formed as a consequence of the transferred atoll meeting its first continental profit-maker.

Nor is this intended as a derogatory assessment. It is simply an explanation of an extremely difficult problem arising from the Austronesian background.

7 Government

Rule by council of elders was the form of government most current among the atoll communities which settled in Asia. It is a form of government integral to atoll society, the most typical form, and the most ancient.

In order to understand it, it is first necessary to understand the building in which it assembled, the two being structurally inseparable.

On every atoll the largest building is the *manéapa*, or hall of assembly, which has to be large enough to seat with reasonable comfort every man, woman and child in the community it serves and represents. On small atolls, as in the Ellice Islands, one *manéapa* often suffices for the whole population. On larger atolls, such as Tárawa in the Gilberts, where it is more than a day's journey from one end of the atoll to the other, there is a *manéapa* for each section of the atoll strip of land, each *manéapa* representing a community, or in continental terms, a neighbourhood. An operative factor in the siting of a *manéapa* is whether it is within walking distance for women and small children.

A Gilbertese *manéapa* is an enormous wooden building with a roof of leaf thatch. In shape it is like a large old English hay barn. From outside, the only noticeable feature is its long gable roof, the eaves of which come down to less than four feet from the ground – one has to bend to the knee to go in. When a breeze is blowing, the lowness of the eaves contributes to creating a cool current of air within. At all times of day, well protected from the sun's heat except just at sunset, it is cool, though when there is no breeze it can become rather stuffy.

Within, it is structurally undivided, one enormous room with a high, gabled ceiling. Being oblong, and having aisles on the outer sides of the main posts which support it, it is unexpectedly like a wood-and-leaf-thatch cathedral, with the wooden posts as the columns of the nave.

To facilitate the advanced courses in astronomy which were formerly conducted in it, a *manéapa* is sited according to the points of the compass. To pursue the cathedral simile, the altar would be in the north, the nave being laid out north to south, with aisles on the east and west. It can be entered from any side, being open all round, except that by convention guests enter and leave from the west.

The Gilbertese are divided into what are called clans, though the use of this word can be misleading. They are groups of families with a common male ancestry. They do not have the property structure of a Chinese clan.

At the time of the last invasion, members of the clan of the Sun might have established, along with other clans, a foothold in three separate parts of a large atoll. Between these three parts of one clan there would be no mutual property interest, unless they were linked additionally by marriage, in which case property might come into it.

This form of clan structure, being related more to ancestry than to property, is comparatively weak. When transferred to Asia, among intensely conservative groups such as those who settled in Japan, it survived, as it did among the Gilbertese, whose ancestors were settled in the Moluccas. Elsewhere, the clan structure being small, and for geographical reasons divisible, the clans tended to dwindle away into unimportance, succumbing to distance, the distances between division and division of the same clan being far greater in Asia than they were between one neighbourhood and another on an atoll.

In Asia the social element which established itself, and endured, was that of the arrival group in the boats, those who were the founders (together with the local people they settled amongst) of the transferred atoll. This feature is reflected in the Philippines in the fact that the *barangay*, the typical rural group, is also the name of the kind of craft they arrived in. Such arrival craft would have included men and women of several clans.

The number of posts, or columns, in a *manéapa* naturally dictates its size, which was determined by the number of clans represented in any given community, there being one post for each clan.

Every man being a landowner, a clan could be said to represent a land interest. In modern terms, the essence of atoll government was that, albeit in minuscule, it represented regional interests, each designated by a wooden post.

The interior of a *manéapa* is carpeted with pandanus fronds, footwear is removed before entering, and there are no chairs. At the foot of each post, facing the nave, sits the head of the clan which the post represents. He will usually sit cross-legged, and being often an elderly man, the position is comfortable, having the post to lean back on.

The senior clans sit in the north, at which end there will probably be four posts. Clan seniority is largely determined by ancient seniorities in the Gilbertese ancestral homeland, which was Samoa. It is in addition determined partly by which clans spearheaded the seizure of that particular section of the atoll at the time of the last invasion, which was when they all first sat down in the new *manéapa*.

Apart from the four senior clans, who have slightly more responsibility in the guidance of affairs, clan seniority is not a live issue. There is no such thing as a junior clan. All are equal, with the exception that the shape of the building dictates that, when guidance is required, it carries greater weight when coming from the end of the building than from halfway down it, just as in the world of today, if a chairman wishes to ensure he carries his committee with him, if he is wise he sits at the head of the table, not in the middle.

When the elders meet in council, the whole of the centre of the *manéapa* – the whole of the nave – is empty. Those who wish to listen to the proceedings sit wherever they can in the aisles, *behind* the elders, and behind the posts. At any important session the aisles are jampacked with people of both sexes and all ages.

When an elder speaks, he does so from his cross-legged seated position, and he continues till he has said what he has to say. No interruption is permissible, being contrary to etiquette. The hall being very large, there has to be silence while an elder is speaking, and he has to speak clearly, or he will not be heard by those distant from him.

There is no chairman. When an elder finishes his speech, there is a pause, lasting at least half a minute. During this pause those who wish to speak next sit quietly, endeavouring to detect among the assembly indications of others of similar intent. No one signals to anyone; no one noticeably moves.

Then, by innate apprehension of the moment, *one* begins to speak. The case of two beginning at once by accident is unheard of, except in understandable cases where an elder is either a little deaf or short-sighted. Such is the degree of care taken to avoid what would otherwise, without a chairman, be an irreconcilable situation.

Here one is in the presence of the most ancient parliament on earth, untold thousands of years old. No one who has witnessed it can fail to be aware of this as its procedure is observed. The degree of wisdom exhibited, based on restraint and respect for others, and the conduct of it, dependent on an advanced state of collective instinct, is unlike that of any other gathering at which contrary opinion is expressed.

On a serious issue, moreover, contrary opinion is expressed often with force, ever with skill in exposition and argument.

It sounds in general a solemn conclave. In essence it is. Wit is seldom absent for long, though. When it takes the upper hand, the *maneapa* can resound to roars of laughter, this being a permissible form of interruption – the only one. Even amid hilarious debate, however, the same procedure of pause and assessment of the moment is followed – as it were, a cooling-off period after each speech.

By permission, any adult male seated in the aisles may take part in debate. When this happens, the man makes his speech standing, addressing the hall from a position in the front row of those seated in the aisles. Only the elders speak seated.

If a man goes on too long, or starts talking nonsense and people become restive, his own elder, or others near, will tell him to sit down and keep quiet. This is never done until there is instinctive consensus that the man is getting nowhere.

Maneapa government is founded in consensus. Debate continues, no matter how long it takes, until there *is* consensus. On a serious issue this takes a long time. Arguments are slowly whittled down, conflicting points reconciled in agreeable compromise, or eliminated by the blandishments of reason. At last a decision, or formula, is reached which is acceptable to all.

There is no concept of majority or minority, no such thing as a casting vote. Majority rule leaves of necessity a dissatisfied minority, which in the tight conditions of an atoll is a deadly danger.

In the Gilberts today, people put it in simple English words – 'Majority rule is not fair.' Which on an atoll it is not. An atoll community either agrees, or disintegrates into the humanly un-endurable.

As debate continues on a serious issue, the same instinctive feelings indicate the stage matters have reached. All can sense it as consensus draws near, even among those elders who may have said nothing. It becomes clear to everyone, and can be exciting. Then, unexpectedly, one of the elders – it might be anyone – utters a sentence which crystallizes the entire issue, and next moment the atmosphere in the *maneapa* indicates that agreement has been reached. One or two speeches may follow in praise of the formula or decision, allowing for it to be certain that agreement is complete. Then, after the usual pause, one of the four senior elders will formally announce the decision, the terms of which thus become binding on all.

Though anyone from the aisles may with permission speak – and in the case of a good speaker with important points to make, his words will receive their full measure of attention – it is the responsibility of the elders to steer matters into consensus. Unlike democratic parliamentarians, whose aim in debate is to reach a representative *division*, a Gilbertese elder enters the *maneapa* in the knowledge that, however obdurate the issue, and however forcefully he intends to present his own views on it, his ultimate responsibility is to bring about unanimous agreement.

The fact that there is no chairman adds weight to this awareness of responsibility. There is no one who can interrupt him, no authority which can overrule him. Each elder is his own chairman, with a chairman's responsibility in addition to that of a member.

Note the significance of the fact that the elders speak from a seated position – and not seated on chairs either, but on the floor, usually cross-legged. As any statue of the Buddha shows, this is a position of calm. Though a man may express himself in choice and pithy words, even in harsh words, they are words weighed, the position they are spoken from being essentially reflective.

Fiery oratory is inescapably related to the standing position. By the ancient device of speaking from the cross-legged position on the ground, an element of restraint and calm is self-imposed on even the most bitter circumstances of debate, which in a *manéapa* is more *considered* than in a Western-style parliament, a feature dictated by the cross-legged position.

Magnificent moments, so dear to politicians but so empty, such as flinging papers on the floor and resigning, or crossing the floor of the house with the drama of an Irving crossing the stage, are precluded on an atoll. For an elder to leave his place would symbolize that his clan had forfeited their land. Florid gesture is likewise precluded; from the cross-legged position it looks ridiculous. Repartee is precluded. Everything is geared to maintain the maximum of calm.

Note too the importance of the fact that each elder, being obliged to sit at the foot of one of the posts supporting the building, is separated by distance from those on either side of him. It is impossible for two elders to murmur to one another in undertones; they are too far apart. One elder cannot even make a gesture or signal to another without attracting the attention of all in the *manéapa*, leading everyone to smell a rat in the proceedings. As the assembly is constructed, each elder sits exposed in his own individual solitude. Every word spoken is a word for all to hear; there is no possibility of anything being done *sub rosa*.

Nor can any party or group effectively form. To be effective, a group must sit together. Were a group to form on an atoll, in the *manéapa* the elders composing it would almost certainly find they were all sitting in the wrong positions, rendering them totally ineffective. Seating, determined by tradition, is unalterable.

These were the methods used to keep intrigue out of public affairs. An elder might be an intriguer in land matters or some other feature in daily life. If he was, in the *manéapa* he was powerless. By the very physical formation of the council, an intriguer gives himself away so quickly, due to each elder's total and separate exposure, that a man who attempted to insinuate an intrigue would condemn himself outright in the face of his entire community.

This was the classic form of government which the atoll people brought with them into Asia. It is the political aspect of the social system known in Indonesia as *gotong royong*, and in the Philippines as *baydnihan*, which means cooperation by consensus, often loosely (inaccurately) rendered as 'mutual cooperation'. To use Indonesian terminology, it is government by *mushuarah* (general discussion by all concerned), leading to *mufakat* (unanimous agreement), on the strength of which a decision is taken which thereby becomes binding on all.

The decision, being unanimous, embodies an oath of obedience. Such is the age of the system that in the Gilberts the oath was implied. Hallowed time rendered the actual saying of it unnecessary.

In Asia, where Pacific clans in general lost their identity, and where in any case many communities represented fusions of Pacific and Asian culture, the special significance of the posts in the assembly hall ceased to be a factor. In the transferred atoll the meeting place was simply a large wooden building in which everyone could sit and talk matters out. The principle of consensus, however, remained.

After chiefs came into existence, this system endured in Insular Asia so long as a chief was recognized as *primus inter pares* among his fellow-elders. Its undermining began with the arrival of Brahminical Hinduism. The subsequent evolution of kings as divine emanations dealt the system a fatal blow, from which it never recovered.

At village level it sometimes survived; and in remote places, where it was out of the clutches of kings, it did so till a recent date. William Marsden, in his great classic, *The History of Sumatra*, published in 1783, noted its existence a few years prior to that date among the remoter Sumatran peoples on the Indian Ocean side of the island.[1]

[1] It is of note that the two foremost political thinkers in the islands, José Rizal (1861–96) of the Philippines, and Sukarno (1901–70) of Indonesia, both believed that consensus was an indispensable principle in all that concerned government and organization among their people. In both countries an attempt to introduce democracy failed. In the Philippines it was replaced (1972) by presidential rule. In Indonesia it has been succeeded by rule of association of functional groups, with the aim of achieving a modern form of rule by consensus. This is the most important political development to have taken place in South-East Asia since the end of the colonial epoch.

PART IV

An Account of Prehistory

Like a huge Python, winding round and round
  The rugged trunk, indented deep with scars
  Up to its very summit near the stars,
A creeper climbs, in whose embraces bound
  No other tree could live.

         TORU DUTT (1856–77): *Our Casuarina Tree*[1]

---

[1] From *Ancient Ballads and Legends of Hindustan*, by Toru Dutt, published post-humously; Kegan Paul, London, 1881.

8 Austronesia in the Pacific

to *circa* 3500 B.C.[1]

The Pacific Ocean covers nearly half the world's surface. For convenience, geographers have divided it into three regions, with names derived from Greek.

Polynesia – *polu*, many, *neesos*, an island – is, as its name states, a region of many islands and atolls. These lie east of the international date line. Hawaii and other islands within striking distance lie north of the equator. The largest concentration of islands lies to the south of it, all within the tropics. It includes Tahiti, Samoa, Tonga, and most of the better-known islands of the Pacific.

Micronesia – *micros*, small – consists of exceptionally small islands and atolls, many of them widely separated one from another. This region lies west of the international date line and north of the equator. It includes the Marianas, the Carolinas, and the Marshalls.

Melanesia – *melas*, black – is the Pacific's most substantial region in terms of land. Consisting mainly of mountainous islands, with few atolls, it stretches from New Guinea, which is usually classified as the world's second largest island, eastward and south-eastward along a chain of islands lying roughly parallel with the north-east coast of Australia, from which the mean distance is some 1,200 miles.

[1] In the succeeding chapters, rather than argue the merits of each statement made, I have chosen instead to state simply what I think happened in the past. Fully to explain why each statement is made would entail a very different kind of book, comprehensible to none save a virtual handful of experts.

The reason I have chosen this form of exposition is this. At the present time in Pacific and South-East Asian studies there is such a multitude of detailed works, and such a paucity of general evaluations, that a stage has been reached where, in the special subject of the prehistoric relations between the Pacific and Asia, scarcely anyone can see the wood for the trees. At such a moment it is sometimes a help to research if someone gives a general evaluation, as clear and simple as possible.

Between the Melanesian chain and Australia lies the Coral Sea, twice the size of the Mediterranean, and about the most dangerous sea on the planet.

Whereas Polynesia and Micronesia are geographical descriptions, Melanesia is a geo-ethnic term – islands with black people on them – the Melanesians belonging to a different race, which has no connexion with the brown-skinned people east and west of them.

Ethnically, but not geographically, Melanesia extends westward from New Guinea, embracing Timor and parts of the Moluccas. Flores, still further west, is partly Melanesian. On the Pacific side, eastward from New Caledonia and the New Hebrides, where the Melanesian chain ends, it has an ethnic outpost in Fiji.

Melanesia therefore lies partly in Oceania, partly in Asia. When the Austronesian world was at its zenith, embracing Oceania and Southern Asia, Melanesia was in a central position, separating the Pacific Austronesians from their distant relatives in Asia. It was this factor which, around 3000 B.C., led to the Austronesian world being severed into two parts, Oceanic and Asiatic, each losing memory of the other.

There was a time in the past – around 15,000 B.C., to give a rough idea – when two-thirds of habitable Oceania south of the equator was peopled by Melanesians, along with others. Over a period of millennia Melanesia has slowly contracted ethnically, and is still doing so on its Asiatic side. In addition to Melanesians, there were pygmies, at least in the Western Pacific, and a white race whose men were bearded and had red hair. Racially the region was more varied than it is today.

Among these races the Melanesians, themselves an amalgam of earlier people of whom traces are obscure, were predominant, this being an age of Melanesian culture, which in the Pacific is represented by the pig and the taro, both integral to the Melanesian way of life.

The story of the Pacific can be condensed into few words: pressures of population, or the search for a better island. At a time when elsewhere in the world men were few, in Melanesia and Oceania men were numerous. The Pacific was the first part of the world to support a large human population.

The Melanesians did not have any organization larger than a village, nor did they have any conception of themselves as branches of a major race. When a Melanesian encountered someone not of his group, though he denoted a likeness, he did not think, 'It is a man'. The word 'man' applied solely to his own group, or tribe. Between his own tribe and others he made an enlarged distinction, much as he would between a pig, a bird or a fish, or between himself and any of these animals. The concept of mankind was absent.[1]

His culture was linked with forested islands, his boat construction dependent on forest timber. On forested islands, such as Fiji, he was well-established; on atolls his tenure was precarious. His social organization was not geared to the tight conditions of atoll life, while the tendency of small groups of Melanesians to quarrel and fight – one outcome of being a race of professional warriors – was a permanent drawback on atolls. When two resident groups on an atoll war with each other, this in atoll life is the ultimate disaster.

The birthplace of the Austronesian civilization lies somewhere in Polynesia. It arose in atolls, not islands, among a brown-skinned people for whom Melanesians were maritally incompatible. A widespread development which took centuries to mature, it achieved its earliest moment of integrated identity in the Tuamotu, the Ancestral Isles – *tua*, old, or pertaining to ancestors, *motu*, segments of land on water, or loosely, islands.

The Tuamotu are an archipelago of atolls, some of them enclosing unusually large lagoons, lying 200 miles and more eastward of Tahiti. Here a people developed a society with atoll equilibrium, a factor which was to prove of great significance. Whereas Melanesians and others could only settle enduringly in Oceania on forested islands, and precariously on better-favoured atolls, the atoll-equilibrated Austronesians could settle more or less anywhere.

With this development of atoll equilibrium came universal ideas, strikingly different from Melanesian ways of thought. Among Austronesians 'man' meant also 'mankind'.

Change as profound as this usually occurs as an outcome of outside contact with compatible people. It is difficult to think of any

[1] See Appendix 2: Melanesian Thought.

human group developing such a radically different way of thought entirely on its own; one suspects here the presence of an untraceable outside influence. If it was an influence which came to the atolls, it became domiciled, learning from the atoll people how to adjust to their social equilibrium. It would otherwise have eliminated itself.[1]

Thirdly, an advanced technology developed. Its features were a language wider and more expressive than the Melanesian languages;[2] improved mathematics brought about by the artificial extension of numerals from five to ten; a prodigious knowledge of astronomy; and in due course the invention of the outrigger, making their vessels, under sail, the fastest known to man prior to the present century, and giving them more stability and staying-power than those of the Melanesians, whose prototype vessel was a dug-out canoe.[3]

This active and ingenious society, enjoying wide contacts in Eastern Polynesia, established a major centre in richly forested Tahiti, where with greater variety of timber its shipping improved and enlarged.[4]

[1] Thor Heyerdahl's epic voyage in the raft *Kon-Tiki* shows how people who had no ocean-going ships could have come from South America and ended up in the Pacific – significantly, in the Tuamotu. And it is worth remembering that when he and his friends reached the Tuamotu, their raft collapsed. They would either learn from the atoll people how to live, or they would die from refusal to learn. I suspect that the Austronesian civilization stems from something similar to Thor Heyerdahl's voyage, and (having no radio with which to send a rescue message) a fusion of cultures.

[2] The Austronesian languages have three features which in combination make them immediately distinguishable. Firstly, the meaning of words is extended by means of affixes and suffixes. Secondly, many nouns and verbs are interchangeable; whether a word is a noun or a verb depends on how it is used in a sentence. Thirdly, all nouns are plural, needing to be qualified by another word to bring them into the singular. This last was the feature which rendered these languages particularly responsive to the expression of universal ideas.

[3] Reference here is, of course, to the *single* outrigger. The double outrigger is the tricycle of the sea.

[4] It is significant that when Captain Cook, after two months' stay in Tahiti, asked the elders where they thought they and their people originally came from, the reply he received was that they had always been there. This in the Pacific is a

From then on, what followed was not so much an extension of people as an extension of knowledge and a way of life. For others who were compatible, the ways of this skilful, modern age of technique and behaviour were attractive, and others adopted elements of it. From island to island Austronesian ideas spread, together with variant forms of Austronesian speech.

In places, pressures of population caused further spread by invasion and conquest, till throughout Polynesia all were related in having kindred languages, ideas and techniques, the whole forming a widely scattered small-island way of life. Despite having no overall organization, it had two particularly evolved centres in Tahiti and Samoa. Though it extended to these relatively large islands, its social forms remained true to their atoll origins.

A feature of Oceanic invasion was that there was scant killing and no slaughter. When an invading force clearly had the upper hand, the resident inhabitants made a *sauve-qui-peut* to their boats, taking their wives and children with them if there was time. Since, with their incredible endurance at sea, they often succeeded in reaching other islands, this caused a further spread of ideas and techniques.

When an invasion was successful, surviving compatible residents were enslaved. Melanesians who survived became downtrodden remnants, left on their own in the wretchedest parts of atolls, from which they in due course either removed themselves if they had boats, or remained dwindling, till they died out. In some places they managed to survive in a depressed condition for a long time. Even at the turn of the present century there were still a few Melanesians in the Northern Gilberts, though now they are no more.

Others more virile, such as the Fijians, resisted territorial encroachment, and carried on with their own way of life. They learned from Austronesians, however, adapting their methods of

---

highly unusual answer, indicating a settlement of great age. Due to the enormous amount of movement in the Pacific, nearly everyone has come from somewhere else (in the Pacific), while due to genealogies, memory reaches back thousands of years. The Tahitian answer tells far more than immediately meets the eye. The name Tuamotu explains itself.

ship-construction, eventually coming to speak an Austronesian language variant.

Outpost Melanesians such as these had connexions further west in Melanesia proper. It was largely through them that Austronesian forms of language gradually spread throughout much of Melanesia, where with the exception of Papua the original languages were all but entirely displaced.

Linguistically, this is the most remarkable achievement of the Austronesian world. An entire race, though they learned little or nothing of new ideas and techniques, adopted the languages which were associated with them, and forgot their own.[1]

This development, first sponsored by Austronesian-speaking Melanesians, was furthered by the continuing westward spread of Austronesians themselves.

These kept their distance from Melanesia proper. Islands such as Bougainville and Guadalcanal, with mountain ranges rising to points over 7,000 feet, did not attract them. Still less did the enormity of New Guinea – or Australia, for that matter.

Well off the coasts of Melanesia, however, there are various lone atolls, some of them large. Ontong Java, lying some 160 miles north of Santa Isabel, in the Solomons, is about the largest of all atolls. In such places Austronesians settled.

Such was the people's prestige that these dots on the ocean map became more important than the substantial islands, including New Guinea, which they embraced like a chain of distant sentinels. In the framework of an ocean civilization, these dots were the centres, mountainous islands the periphery.

The portentous nature of Austronesian arrival on such atolls consisted in the enormity of their personal contacts. Never before or since was there an age when people were so at ease in ocean. Not only had this prestigious people settled on scraps of ocean earth hitherto considered uninhabitable – all seafaring Melanesians knew these atolls – but as if the place was merely another taro garden,

---

[1] It is worth recalling here the Roman saying that the Latin language was worth more than all the legions.

they conducted marriages on a regular basis between other islands which no Melanesian could ever be certain of finding.

As an example, there were regular marriage links between Ontong Java, Ocean Island, and the Gilberts, across 1,000 miles of sheer ocean. Ocean Island is so small it demands calculation within a fraction of one degree to find it. Regular marital relations over such an area are impressive. Today they verge on the incredible. Thus they were seen by Melanesians. The reason for the language change was the prestige of those who spoke it, who included numerous Melanesians.

The penetration of Austronesian language into Melanesia must have taken at least a thousand years, during which the Pacific became an Austronesian ocean. Within the ocean, unconnected with continents, there was diverse movement and intermixture of ideas, customs, and blood. The Pacific remained in an incessant process of social, racial and intellectual change, particularly marked in a centre such as Samoa.

Population throughout this period was high, both in Oceania and Melanesia. As confidence rose in man being master of ocean and such earth as there was, so did population increase. For many young men and women, after a time, there was no land. Short of killing their relatives or neighbours, there was no means of obtaining any.

In the more populous part of Oceania, the direction of search for a better island had always been westward. To those who knew the immensity of ocean, there was more hope to westward, following prevailing winds and currents.

Around 3500 B.C. there was a population explosion in Oceania, one of many. In this case, it was of such dimensions that it projected the search for a better island westward to a pronounced degree. Generally bypassing Melanesia, thrown-out groups of men, women and children – most of the parents probably quite young – threaded their way through the intricacies of the Coral Sea, or penetrated coastally, or on information from atoll to atoll, along the route north of New Guinea, till they reached Asia.

There they found that, in infinitely easier sailing conditions, Melanesia stretched westward from island to island, as far as certain points, Java notable among them, where different but compatible people were at last encountered.[1]

In the explorations that followed, the Asiatic connexion with the Pacific eastward current (known in Oceania) was discovered, providing the return route to the atolls via Micronesia. News slowly went back to Oceania of favourable lands lying to westward. Impetus was given to an increased number of westward voyages, in search of what had come to figure as El Dorado.

This point marks the zenith of the Austronesian civilization, when for a period which probably did not last more than two or three hundred years, there was communication back and forth between Asia and the Pacific, embracing a tropical region which came to extend from Madagascar to Tahiti.

Everyone across this stupendous region – everyone who travelled – spoke different languages which could be bridged. All had similar ideas about ceremonial trade, with similar motives for this. All who were educated – as many were, in terms of education as it was then understood – were aware of being the representatives of man at his most advanced.

It is man's first perceptible essay at greatness.

[1] From the time of the invention of the outrigger – a remote date – it is inevitable that people from Oceania reached Asia by accident, along the 'outrigger route', see fn. p. 68. But these would not have been in sufficient numbers to make a cultural impression on Asia. The indications point clearly to a Pacific population explosion, in the course of which the new arrivals may have found here and there in Asia lone Austronesians who had come by accident.

9 Characteristics of Civilization

The question poses itself whether or not this was a civilization. The fact that, even after its way of life spread from atolls to forested islands, it developed no handwriting or sculpture suggests at first sight that to call it a civilization is to exaggerate.

Handwriting did not develop on atolls because on an atoll there is nothing that could conceivably be written on. There are no suitable leaves, and while it was possible to make dots on pandanus wood with a coral pin, this was as far as human expression went in this direction. Not even stone could be used. On an atoll there is no stone. An advanced culture developed in which learning was dependent solely on memory.

By the time the culture spread to forested islands, memory was so developed, and the culture so self-sufficient, that there was no necessity for writing. Had it occurred to anyone to invent it, it would have been dismissed as superfluous.

The reason sculpture did not develop concerns decorum. The Melanesians in their homelands were great sculptors, using wood and treefern. Such forms of expression did not appeal to Austronesians. Their religion was ancestral, and the ancestors were thought of as real but invisible. A sculpture of the human form, since it was not a human being, inevitably created a mental association with ancestors, to sculpt whom was disrespectful, also damaging, in that it would have the effect of tying them to the earth.[1]

The principal subject of general education was history, children being taught by their grandparents. Every male youngster had to learn to memorize his genealogy. This was not simply a list of names; it included brief relation of important events with which prominent

[1] The ancestral cult was personal to the individual. For a description of it in practice in the Gilbert Islands see Sir Arthur Grimble: *A Pattern of Islands*. Whether in addition there was a group cult is uncertain, probably not, at least in the Pacific.

ancestors were concerned, and their achievements. An average genealogy went back a thousand years. An advanced genealogy went back further than this, though in an inevitably hazy form, till it reached the original clan head, who was created, not born.

Wherever invasions occurred, genealogies were upset, being clear as far as the last invasion, indistinct beyond, though still reasonably serviceable as a historical record. Learned men were familiar with the principal genealogies of their community. These compositely gave a remarkably good general history of the people. When a new elder took his place in the *manéapa* for the first time, he had to recite his entire genealogy, and be subject to questioning by others, to establish in a formal manner his right to the place he was taking.

The universality of Austronesian ideas, which was their most commanding intellectual feature, is best exemplified in their creation stories. Where Melanesian thought contained nothing supernatural or deistic, each Melanesian account of man's origin relating exclusively to a particular tribe in a particular place, Austronesian thought envisaged a Creator who from out of a void created the universe and the world, which was created by 'separating the sea from the sky', after which the first ancestors were set down on small islands. Albeit these stories make no reference to the continental world – in all their versions they are intrinsically aquatic, the continental world being evidently unknown to those who first told these stories – they represent the striking difference that for the first time in Oceania the concept of humanity as a whole has come into existence.

Where this remarkable difference in thinking occurs inexplicably – thus, as it were, suddenly – the development of mathematical thought can be perceived.

To what extent Melanesians could count is not known. When the Austronesian language was born, man counted up to three, language containing only three numerals. In due course, two more were added, the words for four and five being not numerals, but archaic words bearing other meanings. After this, the numbers six to ten were added, these too being archaisms, though less archaic, their meanings more discernible than is the case with four and five. The whole indicates a mental progression from counting in threes, to fives, to tens.

The ability of the mind to encompass a larger considerable unit is the ultimate criterion of that mind's capacity. By the addition of the word 'beyond' – one beyond, two beyond, for eleven, twelve, etc. – a full mathematical system developed.[1]

The principal subjects of higher education, which was confined to a few, were astronomy and navigation.

Their knowledge of astronomy became prodigious, and the subject was scientifically taught. A student of astronomy took the arduous seven-year course in the *manéapa*, without actual reference to the stars – a brilliant device in relation to a people with no handwriting.

Seated in the centre of the *manéapa* floor, the student learned by heart the names, shapes and positions of the stars and constellations by reference to the divisions in the *manéapa* roof, which is divided into rectangles by rafters and purlins. The roof, which falls on both sides almost to the horizon, represented the night sky, with the ridgepole as the meridian.

The student began by learning the state of the night sky at nightfall at the beginning of the year, which was judged by the positions of the Pleiades and the star Antares, the year beginning when the Pleiades were in the first purlin, approximately 15 degrees above the eastern horizon shortly after sundown. Having mastered this, the longest part of the course, he then learned the nocturnal movement of the stars, again in relation to the rectangles in the roof, and after this the seasonal variations. There is nothing primitive about this. It is in the last degree sophisticated and accurate.

In addition, he did a course in seamarks, as opposed to landmarks – the movement of birds, the location of currents, their direction and temperature, the known positions of floating seaweed, certain types of wave, certain types of fish close to the surface, and so on. With his knowledge of seamarks by day and astronomy by night, an experi-

[1] Many languages in Africa have only five numerals, and the earliest Chinese written numerals show that the same once applied in China. The Austronesian languages are, so far as I know, the only ones to give a clear indication of a time when man counted only up to three; it is suggestive of their immense age.

enced Austronesian navigator could tell at any time where he was as accurately as a ship's captain today.[1]

There are various moments in the study of Austronesia when one detects the existence of an unknown genius somewhere in the far past. This is one such moment. Whoever invented that method of teaching astronomy was a master mind. Reflecting on the fact that the *manéapa*, the most important building on an atoll, had to be specially sited according to the points of the compass in order to facilitate the teaching of astronomy, one would imagine the master mind to have been a person of some consequence and influence.

Beside their astronomy and navigation must be set their ship-construction. The few prehistoric ships which survived into the European period served to give an idea of the size and strength of vessels in former times. It was not unusual for a vessel to be eighty feet in length, with a fifty-foot outrigger. These ships were every whit as seaworthy and larger than the caravels with which the Portuguese discovered the sea route to India, and under sail they moved much faster. When one reflects that they were constructed with coral implements, an extremely lengthy and demanding task, they were in fact masterpieces of technology.

To this must be added the undisputed tradition that this was a time of peace. Conflicts there undoubtedly were, and invasions. This is not what has been chiefly remembered. Peace was the real hallmark of this age.

Another point concerns religion – again, the evidence is from the Gilbert Islands prior to their evangelization.

There was much diversity of religious view in the Austronesian world. Different clans held to different traditional explanations of religious matters, on a scale which would quickly have plunged Europe into war. Yet there was no religious controversy. Linked with *manéapa* tradition and procedure, there was ingrained tolerance with regard to contrary opinion. This is a mark of civilization.

Most salient of all, however, is the contemporary fact, visible in the remarkable spread of Austronesian languages among unrelated

[1] For a full account of these courses as they were formerly conducted in the Gilbert Islands, see Rosemary Grimble, *op. cit.*

people, that those who belonged to this culture and way of life were *seen* by others as civilized and superior. Their civilization differed from later human efflorescences in having no large-scale organization, no paramount chiefs, still less kings. Chiefs were temporary, being leaders and promoters of expeditions. Once an atoll or island was settled, the *maneapa* dictated behaviour; and in a *maneapa*, while there is a place for seniority, there is none for a chief.

IO   The Melanesian Reaction

circa 3000 B.C.

The zenith of the Austronesian world is the period described in Melanesia as the Great Peace. Though it is improbable that this extended throughout all Melanesia, linguistic evidence indicates that it certainly extended to smaller islands which came within the orbit of Austronesian activity.

Every Melanesian man was trained as a warrior, mostly by gruelling methods. War was a professional science, as too was cruelty. In many tribes there were learned men who in modern terminology would be called professors of cruelty. In addition, there were the sorcerers, who were always among the main instigators of war, from which they benefited in power and prestige. Unless Melanesian society could make some drastic adaptations, it was unlikely that the Great Peace could last.

Around 3000 B.C., in conditions for which Austronesians were themselves partly responsible, it ended in a violent reaction of anti-pathy to the intrusion of outsiders.

Apart from language, the Melanesians had learned little from the Oceanic people. Oceanic religious ideas, with their universal basis, were beyond the Melanesian mind. They did not improve their navigation by the study of astronomy. They did not even adopt the outrigger. Beside this, being a black race, they were considered unmarriageable, a condition acting as a brake to the transmission of ideas. They had in fact become a backward people, and were evidently being treated so by those who sailed through their waters.

The immediate cause of the collapse of Austronesia, however, which followed as a consequence of the Melanesian reaction, was concerned with theft.

The atoll people, with their relaxed approach to borrowing and lending, and their subtly diminished sense of personal property, have nearly everywhere been regarded as thieves. When encountering unrelated people among whom theft was not a capital crime, precautions were taken by the latter, and relations were not unduly impaired.

In Melanesia theft was held in singular abhorrence, being considered a shameless act. In Asia, wherever the atoll people settled on Melanesian islands where the population was sufficiently low for another community to establish a separate foothold – as on Bali – the outcome was a Melanesian withdrawal from contact, to get away from what they regarded as pilfering.

In Melanesia proper, densely populated and culturally adamant, when Austronesians, amid conditions of deteriorating race relations, ignored with Melanesians the conventions of ceremonial trade etiquette, came ashore, and seized what they required in the way of food for the next stage of their journey into Asia, the reaction was violent.

Melanesian ideas of *mana* were more pronounced than in Polynesia. It is possible that *mana* is in origin a Melanesian concept. An island or a tribal land in Melanesia had *mana* of its own. Nothing, not even a pebble, could be taken away from it without damaging the soul-substance of the land and the people who lived there – a matter to which great importance was attached. In addition, to steal anything strong in *mana*, such as pigs and taro, filled people with a sense of unspeakable anguish.

News has always travelled fast in Melanesia, at sea due to the amount of inter-island travel, on land due to the drum code, which is the closest thing these islands have to a common language, and is highly efficient and quick.[1] Relatively few incidents of thieving would be sufficient to provoke a 'national' reaction along all coasts.

At this time, Austronesian vessels carried here and there men who, having returned to the Pacific via Micronesia, were making the journey through Melanesian waters for the second time, probably with a devil-may-care attitude to the local inhabitants, westward of

[1] In 1942, under Japanese occupation the Solomon Islanders revived the drum code to transmit intelligence to the secret British headquarters on Malaita. It took 20 minutes for messages to be transmitted 50 miles. The code has the advantage that it surpasses differences of language and dialect.

whom lay better lands and fairer women. This could have been one of the factors causing a worsening of relations.

In any event, within a short time these became coasts of inveterate hostility to outsiders. Every attempt to replenish supplies ended in vicious conflict.

These were voyages on which married men were bringing their wives and children. As word slowly spread back to the Pacific concerning the dangers of Melanesia, the westward movement of people from the Pacific into Asia lessened and dried up. Population pressure having eased for the moment, there was probably in any case less real demand for this movement.

The Melanesian reaction sundered the Austronesian world in two. The Pacific Ocean thereupon relapses into 4,500 years of oblivion, from which scholars today, and such pioneer investigators as Thor Heyerdahl, are gradually disinterring it.

Melanesian resistance to outsiders was probably the work of one or two coastal groups acting on their own. They undoubtedly expressed the unspoken will of a people and of an age plunged into bitter disillusion with a changing world. The Melanesians, in a mental climate of rejection, enveloped themselves in a narrowed-down version of the former age, in which to some extent they had been masters. With ancient rivalries resurrected, they resumed their strangely static tribal wars. Since none from outside came near them, they gradually forgot that anyone existed other than themselves.

From this point, in conditions in which each tribe or group held its own small area of land, of which every limit, even including the sea, was potentially hostile, the Austronesian-derived languages of Melanesia began to fissiparate into an infinitude of dialect, each the outcome of its own isolation in an environment of near-total hostility, producing eventually the conditions of today, in which there are more languages and dialects in Melanesia than in any other part of the world.[1]

---

[1] Where other Austronesian languages developed and changed in response to outside stimuli, the Melanesian variants hardly changed at all. They thus reflect the earliest forms of surviving Austronesian speech. The history of the languages of Polynesia and Insular Asia cannot be understood without a knowledge of Melanesian grammar and vocabulary. See Appendix 3: Language and War in Melanesia.

5. Bali: an example of the tiered pagoda which seems to date from megalithic times.

A Land Dayak 'bachelor' house in Borneo; ship motifs are a recurring feature in the architecture of South-East Asia.

6. '. . . the most spectacular of all Asia's irrigation works' – the rice terraces of the Ifugao people in the Mountain Province, Luzon, Philippines. The author dates these to the period of Old Hinduism (eighth to third centuries B.C.) and ascribes the outer influence connected with them to Indonesia rather than to China.

II Austronesia in Asia

Asia, as the atoll people discovered it, differed notably from today in its racial components. Melanesia, which now has its western outposts in Halmahera, Amboina, and eastern Flores, extended westward to Celebes, and through the Indonesian archipelago as far as Bali, which was a Melanesian island, and perhaps even as far as East Java.

Indians and Chinese were unknown, as were the Burmese, the Thai and the Vietnamese, all of whom were living further north, in what is now China. But here and there the newcomers found compatible people, the Torája, the Dayak, the Batak, and others of whom there is no trace (because they 'married them out'); and perhaps most notable of all, the ancestors of the people who later came to be known as the Mon and the Khmer, with whom in particular they intermarried.

They were everywhere welcomed. This is a feature which the Western mind, conditioned to thinking of ancient times in terms of savagery, finds it difficult to grasp. It is an indisputable fact. Basic to it is that, while in Oceania population was dense, in Asia it was sparse.

The clearest evidence of this feature is to be found in the Philippines, the story of which, prior to the coming of the Spaniards, could be called a saga of peaceful arrival. For thousands of years small groups of people kept arriving from other places, motivated by the search for better places to live, and by plain Pacific adventurousness. It was in addition a time of extensive travel, of which the principal feature was ceremonial trade.

Two boatloads of people from Borneo would arrive at some remote spot on Mindanao or Luzon. After some difficulties they would soon find they could make themselves understood by the local people. Where visitors of this kind settled ashore, it was often because they had a superior skill to impart, making them not only welcome but useful. They might be able to make an advanced type of fishtrap, or a stake-net, or hammocks, or they might be better boatbuilders. Starting as a small separate colony, they would gradually tone into the landscape and assume the local common identity.

For thousands of years this kind of thing went on all over South-East Asia, producing the curious condition that while cultures, tribal and otherwise, remained everywhere distinctive and diverse, physical appearance took a move from diversity towards conformity, producing a general South-East Asian physical type amid which, despite anything a presumed expert may say, it is extremely difficult to tell by physical appearance to which group anyone belongs.

This stands in marked contrast with Polynesia, where while culture, dictated by the tight conditions of geography, is relatively uniform, physical appearance denotes instantly which group of atolls or islands anyone comes from.

In South-East Asia the only people excluded from this mingling of peoples were the black-skinned Melanesians and various aborigines, who remained as they were, physically and to a great extent culturally also.

In the earliest stages the intermingling of peoples was aided by the almost infectious ease with which Pacific languages can be learned. Movement and resettlement of people was always on a small scale at any given moment. Its large-scale effects were due to its taking place continuously over a long period of time.

Once any community established itself in Asia with a Pacific-derived language, such languages tended to become geographically static. Thus, for instance, the recently arrived Sumatran Malay colony which was still discernible in the Manila region when the Spaniards first arrived, ended by speaking the local Tagálog, eventually losing all trace of a separate identity, and becoming Tagál.

The static positioning of languages has given many inquirers the impression that they are dealing with different races, or branches of races, whose origins they have endeavoured to trace on the basis of composite groups with a common background. No such approach is tenable. None of these people are races, or branches of races, in that sense, not even the tribal people. They are cultural and linguistic fusions of people whose ways have become sufficiently entrenched to demand adaptation on the part of a newcomer.

Physically they are the outcome of thousands of years of casual movement and resettlement, movement which is continuing all the time, even today, though the numbers involved are so small as to render this indiscernible. Three small families may for some reason move into a tribal area and become tribal; elsewhere tribal people may come down to a coast and become coastal, adopting the culture of the region, in the end becoming indistinguishable from others around them.

The people of the region as a whole are often described as mongoloid, giving the erroneous impression that their ancestors must at some remote date have moved southward from continental Asia. There is no evidence of any such movement.[1] Such 'mongoloid' characteristics as exist are dictated largely by geography, which exerts on human appearance a physical influence entirely its own, and partly by fortuitous crossbreeding over a period of thousands of years, in the later part of which there was indeed, among certain people, a mongoloid admixture.

With such a mingling of people there was an inevitable mingling of cultures. Nearly everyone borrowed something from someone else, while adhering basically to their own tribal or other customs. This has compounded the difficulty of studying these cultures today. There are instances where a newly arrived Pacific group developed such close contacts with an indigenous people that they actually divided into the earlier dual society of hill and coast, making it quite impossible nowadays to tell who is really who.

Creation and origin stories underwent changes, and these changed versions are the only ones that have survived. Occasionally they have

---

[1] The contention, endlessly repeated in contemporary writing, that early mankind reached his present whereabouts on foot over the land bridges that are thought to have once linked the islands with continental Asia is based on surmise. Early man's cultural similarities in this region relate more to time than to movement.

been taken by researchers to be original stories, resulting in some strange conclusions.

As an example of the snares a researcher has to watch out for, there is a story among the Land Dayaks of a giant winged personage who in some versions stepped across from Sumatra to Borneo, in other versions flew. This has been taken to suggest that the Land Dayaks originally reached Borneo by way of Sumatra. They themselves do not draw any such deduction from the story, considering they have always lived more or less where they are now.

Throughout this part of the world, if anyone in a story becomes airborne it is a sign that the story is of Hindu origin. Hindu stories have the peculiarity that they are the only ones in which prehistoric man sometimes flies. That Dayak story, in other words, does not relate to origins or first arrival. It belongs to a later period, when there was Hindu influence in Borneo. Snares such as this have to be constantly watched for.

Meanwhile, to make matters more complicated, most of the Pacific people ended by forgetting their Pacific origins. After they lost contact with the Pacific, it was not long before there was no one in Asia who had ever experienced that immense ocean. Though they probably knew for a long time that they came from islands to the east, this in Asia could easily mean from Celebes or the Moluccas. In most of their languages no distinction was made between an atoll and an island; both were islands, and they would come to be judged by such islands as were known in Asia. At the same time, knowledge of astronomy dwindled, being of less importance in the easier conditions of Asian sailing. Men lost all idea of quite how far away those islands of theirs to the east were.

Even today it is almost impossible to explain the realities of the Pacific to anyone who has not seen it. Because no one who had not seen it could ever imagine it, the Pacific was forgotten.

Genealogies, which might have kept open an avenue to the past, underwent changes similar to those that attend an atoll invasion – accurate up to the time of Asiatic settlement, becoming hazy beyond this. With the decline in clan consciousness, due to the 'weak' structure of Pacific clans, interest in genealogy waned, till a time came when only a few traditionalist families remembered theirs, and these only in relation to Asia.[1]

The ancestral character of religion endured; but with the unimaginable Pacific withdrawn from memory, the islands which witnessed the creation of the first ancestors became Asiatic islands, while the ancestors themselves became Asiatic ancestors.

[1] As, just possibly, in the case of the Japanese Emperors.

12 Society in the Melanesian Age

Melanesia, except for its extreme ethnic fringes in Indonesia and Fiji, remained in a state of total isolation from around 3000 B.C. till A.D. 1567, when Mendaña discovered the Solomon Islands, and in virtual isolation till the arrival of British traders and missionaries in the 1830s.

This period of isolation having been inaugurated on a revivalist note, internal social change, though there was some, was slight. Melanesia stewed in its own juice for some five thousand years. As a result, when first examined by philologists and ethnographers, it presented a spectacle of daily life bearing a marked resemblance to living conditions in 3000 B.C., where these had not *deteriorated*.[1]

These living conditions were not special to Melanesia. In this part of the tropical world they related to all mankind, regardless of skin colour, wherever human life was settled in social groups under constructed roofs.

Parallel in time with this form of culture was another in which man lived beneath unconstructed roofs, mainly in caves. Except among mere handfuls of people, the culture of the unconstructed roof died out, leaving the impression that it was a form of life which preceded that of the constructed roof. In fact, the two were contemporaneous. In many places, notably in Melanesia, the constructed shelter, built with poles and leaves, was the only form of human dwelling.

Though some in the region had wandering tendencies, both on land and sea, none were nomads. Here, unlike human development in much of Eurasia, the culture of the constructed roof represents original man.

[1] As, with the introduction of head-hunting in the Solomons, for example, they had, and comparatively recently. Head-hunting does not seem to date from earlier than the fifteenth century A.D. See my *Western Pacific Islands*, Chap. 12.

Melanesia having provided modern man with the most detailed impression of early human life, the pre-Austronesian period is being referred to here as Melanesian, even though it applied to all races in the region, wherever there was a constructed roof. Though this form of human life is considered at the time of Austronesian impact, it is immensely older than this.

Man and pig

The most obvious characteristic of human culture in the Melanesian period was its small-scale diversity. Surviving Melanesian culture, in Melanesia itself, is bewilderingly diverse, and Melanesian physical appearance is scarcely less so. Indeed, the further back one reaches into man's past in Melanesia and South-East Asia, the more diverse does man seem to have been.

But through all this small-scale diversity there ran through human life certain similarities of an almost formalistic nature, relating to the condition of man as he was at that time, taking no account of differences of colour or language.[1]

The first of these was the common condition that settled culture was everywhere based on man and pig. In other parts of the world the dog is thought of as man's first animal friend. Here there were no dogs. Man's true friend in the animal world was the pig, the relationship between them arising from the special pleasure the pig takes in consuming human defecation. This not only solved a hygiene problem in man's early settlements, but created a bond of affection between the two. Here was an animal which admired of man precisely what he himself found revolting, a quality which aroused his appreciation of the pig.

Earlier it was seen how Melanesians made an enlarged distinction between themselves and others not of the tribe, and other animals. As a corollary to this, they made a much reduced distinction between themselves and their own animals, in particular the pig, who was intimately a part of home, whether the pig lived in it,

---

[1] As an example, the racial difference between a Land Dayak of Borneo and a Solomon Islander is, in its Asian context, quite as marked as that between a Nigerian and a Dane.

beside it, or underneath it. A pig was strong in *mana*, almost a person. Such was the closeness of the relationship that until quite recently, well within this present century, there were parts of Melanesia where a mother who had lost a newborn child would think nothing of easing her breasts by nourishing a piglet.

Outside Melanesia the closeness between man and pig was widened by later and more 'enlightened' influences. To this day, though, wherever there is man-and-pig culture, as among the Dayaks of Borneo and many others, this is man in his earliest settled condition of which there is trace in this region.

The criteria of man's estimate of the pig varied. In some places he was esteemed for his tusks, which were allowed to grow by knocking out the eye teeth of a pig when young. Elsewhere he was esteemed in numbers, whether fat or thin, and in other places for size and strength. This esteem did not preclude his being eaten, though in general pigs were only killed and eaten on ceremonial occasions.

Hill and coastal

The next feature of the formal pattern of human life was the division into separate hill and coastal people, the geographical determinant here being the quality of water.

Uniformly throughout this great region, wherever the spring and mountain water ceased to be crystal clear, the hill peoples' domain ended and the coastal peoples' began. This condition was found equally on large islands such as Borneo and Sumatra, and on quite small hilly islands such as the New Hebrides.

On the larger islands, most of the hill people had never seen the sea, and did not know what it was. The Land Dayaks of Borneo are an instance of this. Although these days they know what it is, because it is explained at school, most of them have still never seen it.

On smaller islands, despite the hill people often living within view of the sea, it held no attractions for them. An extreme in this case was to be found on Espiritu Santo in the New Hebrides, where hill people, living within view of the sea on all four sides of them, never until recently descended near it or had anything to do with it, considering it to be poisonous.

This division would not seem particularly mysterious were it not for the fact that in every instance, island by island, and district by district, there is deemed to be a relationship between the two groups. It would not seem to be a marriage relationship, for the simple reason that neither can stand the living conditions of the other. Though occasional cases of runaway love matches there must have been, these would have been rare, and most would have ended in misery.

The relationship is in fact inexplicable, but indisputable. The 'bush' and 'saltwater' people of any one of the Solomon Islands, the Land and Sea Dayaks of Borneo, the hill and coastal people of Celebes and Sumatra, know themselves – or *knew* themselves when first encountered by Europeans – to be related.

A medieval Sumatran song expresses it best, describing the people of the hill and the people of the coast as two brothers, eternally related, yet destined everlastingly to struggle against each other – as for much of the time they did. The inner meaning of the song is not detectable. All that can be said is that this was part of the formal pattern which ran through human life in this region.

Caste

Finally, there was the formal pattern that, regardless of colour and language, all mankind encountered by the Austronesians was divided into two castes, between whom there was no marriage. Members of the upper caste married exogamously into the upper caste of kindred groups, members of the lower caste likewise.

It is impossible to discern a period here when man has *not* been divided into two castes; and these in varying degrees have been perpetuated into the present age. Contemporary society in the Philippines, Indonesia and Malaysia reflects a caste division, without taking account of which these societies cannot be understood, far less provided for in terms of material advance.

The relative size of the two castes in any given group varied from place to place, and was everywhere unequal. In its classic form, society was divided into a 5% upper caste, consisting of chiefs and men and women of chieftainly descent, and a 95% remainder, who were in a sense *owned* by the chief as principal representative of the upper caste and its interests. With this ownership went responsibility for the 95% remainder, also exercised by the chief in the interests of the upper caste.

In parts of Melanesia the castes were represented by symbols – two kinds of hawk, or a lighter and darker kind of coconut. Nowhere did they have names. The reason for this was that they were sacred, thus not to be mentioned.

Caste in man's earliest times was, like magic, related to incentive, which can be artificially stimulated in the negative form of prohibition. There being an absolute prohibition on marriage to 95% of available partners, members of the upper caste were provided with an incentive to marry selectively and wisely, ensuring to each group the safeguard of possessing a small echelon of men with inherited ability to make decisions and exercise command. The preservation of this upper echelon, untainted by indiscriminate breeding, which would have weakened it, had a sacred character.

As time passed, the need for so rigid and extreme a division of society lessened in some places. Occasionally the lower caste produced men of a mental calibre and capacity rivalling the upper caste.

In Melanesia, and in Insular Asia among tribal people, there are instances of prehistoric 'liberalizing movements' unrelated to outside influence. As a result of these, up-and-coming men were permitted some of the privileges of the upper caste, softening the edges of the caste distinction, and lessening the numerical disparity between the two castes.

One such liberalizing movement occurred in parts of the New Hebrides at a time which was still just within memory in the European period. For the first time, commoners' sons were privileged to compete with chieftainly sons in the accumulation of pigs and the holding of ceremonial feasts by means of which men mounted to a higher grade of society. The effect of this was that outstanding commoners rose into the chieftainly caste. Marriage being everywhere exogamous, a liberalizing movement of this nature soon spread.[1]

Wherever the present-day Melanesian castes – they are referred to by ethnographers as 'exogamous moieties' – are reasonably balanced in numbers, this is evidence of prehistoric liberalizing, the two castes having originally been more severely unequal.

Among the Dayaks of Borneo the caste distinction is barely evident – even then it is far from easy to descry – suggesting a prehistoric easing of the caste barrier, an easing to which Christianity and modern education have further contributed.[2]

These, then, were the underlying unities in human life as the Austronesians found it in Asia, unities which ran roughshod through every barrier of cultural diversity and difference of colour: the settled culture of man and pig, the division into 'related' hill and coastal people, and the division of mankind into two mutually unmarriageable castes, classically a 5% chieftainly caste, and a 95% remainder.

---

[1] This important feature of 'liberalizing movements' was first noted in Tom Harrisson: *Savage Civilisation*.

[2] Among the Kayan and Kenyah of Borneo, on the other hand, the caste distinction is clearly marked, though it is not described as caste.

13   Caste and the Transferred Atoll

Asian caste and Pacific slaves
Austronesians having no caste system, it would be expected, with their evident superiority and modernity, that in mingling with these older and more static cultures they would ignore the existence of caste, thereby gently expunging it.

The Pacific, however, was ever the scene of Oceanic invasions and conquests. When a battle was clearly lost, flight into the unknown dangers of ocean, with the possible chance of finding an island, perhaps uninhabited, where he would not be enslaved, was considered more commendable in a man than to stay back and surrender to certain slavery. Nevertheless, at any conquest there were men who hesitated to join the *sauve-qui-peut*, or were not quick enough, and who were enslaved.

Melanesians on atolls were not exactly slaves; they were the down-trodden and ignored. Slaves were compatible Oceanic people, remnants of the population as it was prior to the last invasion.

These slaves succeeded eventually, by one means or another, in acquiring land, from which point they were no longer considered slaves, though in marital arrangements it would be remembered that they once had been. This is a process which thus has three phases: from slavery, the first phase, to acquisition of land, the second phase, to the point where intermarriage with the paramount landowners became socially acceptable, the third phase.

Taking the Gilberts once more as an example, the length of time covered by this process, from the first phase to the third, was roughly four hundred years. Allowing for the fact that, though the tenor of settled Oceanic life was peaceful, it had its interruptive moments of invasion and conquest, at any given moment there would be a certain number of slaves and unmarriageable landowners on virtually any atoll or island.

Except when sailing to Asia in desperate conditions, when slaves might be abandoned, nearly every large Pacific vessel carried a certain number who, though in appearance no different from the rest, were in fact slaves. When settlement started in Asia, and it slowly became known in the Pacific that there were better islands to the west, it is logical to assume that slaves would have been particularly keen to be taken on westward voyages, since for them it afforded an immediate opportunity to obtain land.

The Austronesians, with every shipload that made a landfall in Asia, arrived divided into two classes, landowners and slaves, mutually unmarriageable, a condition strangely similar to the caste division they found wherever they settled among local people. This is an instance where an intrinsically Oceanic feature of life encountered in Asia something which, though of different origin, resembled it, thereby confirming and strengthening that Oceanic feature in its Asian environment.

Arriving – men, women and children – in two ranks (which was what it amounted to), they encountered two castes. The ranks and the castes were different. Where caste at that time was a static condition of human life (as it is in India), difference of rank needed only time and opportunity to make it disappear entirely. On first encounter, though, the two appeared to be the same, the outcome being that rank was confirmed and strengthened by its encounter with caste.

It in fact *became* caste. Albeit the slave element in the Pacific new arrivals acquired land with an ease which would have been impossible on an atoll, they retained their unmarriageable status in respect of their own landed element, which had become a caste. This of itself meant that, whether they liked it or not, the slave element also had become a caste. Nor, having land of their own and compatible women, would they have found any reason to object. They were in fact much better off.

The Philippine barangay *as a typical social structure*
The societies so formed were a mingling of two cultures and two periods of time, man-and-pig and Austronesian; and the girls of the

former were compatible. Pacific elders and atoll landowners fitted into the Insular Asian 5% upper caste, slaves into the 95% lower caste. No other arrangement was considered proper in Asian society.

When, as a result of the coming of trade for profit, chiefs came into existence, and where Asian petty chiefs already in existence survived the introduction of rule by elders, a type of society came into being of which the earliest and most reliable descriptions are to be found in Spanish accounts of the Philippine *barangay*, which is a typical two-caste structure.

As classically described, the *barangay* consisted of the *datu*, or hereditary chieftain, who had three kinds of subjects: freemen, who provided services to the chief; serfs, who surrendered half their crops; and slaves who owned nothing, being themselves owned by someone, usually the *datu*.

This, to a Spanish eye, looked so similar to a European feudal structure that its two-caste nature was not noticed, a situation rendered understandable by the fact that in the Philippines the two castes had no names.

Actually, within his own upper caste the chief was *primus inter pares*. Because of his extra responsibilities he had to be fed and looked after, a function which his so-called 'freemen' – actually his peers – took charge of.

This was interpreted by European commentarists as 'service' of a feudal and compulsory nature, implying that those who gave such service were of a rank lower than the chief. In fact, they were of the same rank, all of them members of the small upper caste. The reason they gave prompt 'service' was that their own upper-caste interests were involved.

Next in the *barangay* came the serfs, the Pacific slave element which became identified with the Asian lower caste, or *ata* – the word most commonly used in the Philippines is *tao*. These were, to their great advantage, landowners in the sense that they owned their houses, the trees, etc., on the land around these, and their domestic animals.

One of the important features which Pacific people adopted from Asians was the communal ownership of land; and the reasons are obvious. It was no longer necessary to depend on the taro as a cereal. In Asia the cereal was hill rice, grown by shifting cultivation – burning hillsides and planting amid the ash, harvesting and moving on to another hillside, leaving the first to lie fallow.

In an area with good soil, one or two years of lying fallow is sufficient before planting the same hillside. In areas of poor soil, as in Borneo, a group might need as much as a ten-year rotational cycle of cultivation.

The use of land on such a scale, even a three-year rotation, was beyond the imagination of Pacific people, who had never conceived of having to deal with so much land. Naturally – often being in the position of superior immigrants among communities already long-formed – they followed existing practice, having nothing comparable from their own background to guide them.

These large expanses of land also had to be protected from intrusion by others, while hill cultivation of rice is essentially a group activity, demanding large numbers of men working in accord, to make the fires effective, and to plant rapidly across substantial areas burnt. Shifting cultivation is in fact inseparable from a certain degree of communal ownership, and totally inseparable from communal identity.

Under this, too, the slave element from the Pacific vessels did remarkably well. Though not individual owners of cereal land (as with a microscopic taro garden on an atoll they might have become), they were joint owners of communal land, with a joint right to half the harvest over an acreage which shifted rotationally from year to year.

When irrigation was introduced, those who had the patience to turn over to it found that their right to cereal-producing land had been enhanced. Though ownership was still communal, cultivation was no longer mobile. This being so, men in their own way sorted the business out, dividing the labour, and giving permanence to these divisions by planting and looking after this year the bunds and fields they dealt with last year. Imperceptibly – though never even to this day throughout most of Insular Asia has this been legally registered – those fields became theirs, though ever in relation to a joint ownership.

Such, then, were the serfs, or *ata*, the remainder or lower caste.

Slaves who owned nothing were not, as has sometimes been supposed, a separate group. They were penalty slaves, men and women who, either they or their forebears, had committed some serious misdeed. Though in theory they could belong to either caste, in practice they were *ata*; and they were marriageable to property-owning *ata*. The child of a penalty slave married to a property-owner became a half-slave, and the children of a quarter-slave became eligible to own property.[1]

In the days of shifting cultivation this meant that the son of a quarter-slave had a right to his share of the produce of the communal land. After irrigation was introduced, the situation for a freed man became more difficult. Unless he could open new fields in a peripheral area, he was often better off doing slave work, becoming in his freed status a domestic servant, with a right to his own house if he could manage to build one.

At the root of the slave system lay one of the major features of Austronesian justice, which was the absence of capital punishment.

The penalty for all justifiable crime – this included murder – was a fine, to be paid in specified kind. For serious crimes the fines were heavy. Any who could not pay, in effect paid with themselves, forfeiting all they possessed, they themselves and their wives and children being reduced to penalty slavery. Where a malefactor had wronged a particular family, he could become that family's slave. In Asia he more commonly became a slave of the chief, or of a member of the upper caste who might ask for his services.

Even in the case of unjustifiable crime, such as (on atolls) incest and adultery, capital punishment was avoided wherever possible. On an atoll, the offending couple would be lashed together with fibres, and put in a boat without sail or paddle, which was then released to the sea on the atoll's leeward side. It almost certainly meant a slow and frightful death. There was always the possibility, though, that luck might deem otherwise. In any case, no one actually executed them.

---

[1] See Morga, *op. cit.*

14 The Age of the Megaliths

circa 1500 B.C. onwards

The Orient of today is formed of five identifiable civilizations. Three of these – China, India and Iran – belonging to history and the present, are accessible to detailed study. Austronesia, the fourth, being prehistoric, monumentless and without handwriting, is less accessible. The fifth, similarly prehistoric and without handwriting, has the peculiarity that though it left innumerable monuments, it is more inaccessible still.

This was a civilization connected with dolmens, megaliths, music, and aesthetics. It also had a distinctive style of architecture in wood and thatch, a feature of which was a tiered pagoda. Musically it left its traces throughout the Indo-Chinese peninsula and in Indonesia. In the Malay peninsula, notably in Negri Sembilan, there are thousands of megalithic remains. It is in the Indonesian archipelago, however, that it left the most durable traces, having a profound general effect on aesthetic thought.

Sometimes referred to as Austric – though with various connotations depending on the user – it is a civilization which has not yet received a name which has stabilized itself. So far as Indonesia and Malaya are concerned, the prime movers in it seem to have been people from another place, though who they were and where they came from are unknown. By about 1500 B.C. the main features of this incoming culture were established along the Indonesian archipelago, from Java to Flores. It endured till at least the fourth century B.C., perhaps later. It will be referred to here as the period of the megaliths.

In the early part of the period the principal remains are dolmens, other related constructions, where there were any, having been in wood and thatch which has not survived. Most of the megalithic structural formations discovered belong to the end of the period, from the fifth century B.C. onwards, when there was a tendency to construct at least the lower parts of edifices in durable materials, and on occasion to use large stones, whence the use of the word mega-lithic.

So little is known of this period that it is being treated here in terms of a single outside influence. In fact, during the thousand years covered by it there was obviously a great deal of development and change, particularly in view of the fact that the period bridges the age of metal. The mentality of the early dolmen phase probably differed considerably from that of the later megalithic, yet the latter is an evolution from the former, and in respect of both, the influence is external.

In that this influence caused no radical alteration in language, it could be that it reached the region through the intermediary of a related people. The languages are so easy to learn, however, that direct external influence cannot be precluded. Nor is it possible to dismiss the likelihood of a direct connexion between the dolmens of Indo-nesia and those of Europe. As mentioned in Part III, Chapter 6, there are indications of an early contact with Mediterranean culture, and that this contact was maintained is suggested by the numerous hints of Phoenician voyages to the East Indies, or at any rate of people regarded as Phoenicians – the name used is *finis*. These indications are found as far east as Celebes and Flores, suggesting that the goal of such voyages was to collect sandalwood from Timor and spices from the Moluccas.[1]

The dolmens of Flores, and the large leaf-shaped stones which are a feature of the upper reaches of the Muar river in Malaya, are alike considered by local people to be the tombs of their ancestors. This factor has hampered investigation, no one being permitted to tamper with the stones. If they are in fact tombs, this has to be related to the Austronesian context. Due to the departed being thought of as real – virtually alive – but invisible, a tomb in the Austronesian world bore a significance unlike that of tombs in Ancient Egypt or Christian Europe. The fact that a tomb contained bones was of minor importance. The essential was that the tomb was

[1] See Appendix 6: Early Trade with Insular Asia.

a symbol of respect for the ancestors, who were real, and could be summoned if necessary.[1]

In parts of Negri Sembilan, in the Malay peninsula, peaceful villages, ricefields, fruit gardens and roadsides are littered with megalithic stones, some of them sculpted and all carved, while the long, narrow island of Flores is a mass of dolmens from end to end. The wide region over which the general remains of the period are scattered indicates that what is left represents only a fragmentary testament to an age of extraordinary constructional activity. These are the first durable constructions to be found in the Austronesian world, and so unexpected is the thought-content which lies behind them, so seemingly remote from the villages of the wood-constructed transferred atoll, that an immediate reaction is to wonder whether local people had anything to do with them.

The influence which the period had on Indonesian thought shows that they did. The arts of Java and Bali cannot be properly understood without taking account of the megalithic period, in which for the first time atoll thought learnt to express itself in constructional form, a kind of expression which does not exist on an atoll, the wherewithal for it being missing.

Construction

The principal feature of megalithic construction could be described in modern terms as landscaping: an ability to see landscape in broad perspective, select key points and formations for what were evidently sacred purposes, and construct in harmony with these natural formations.

As can be seen at once, the idea of atoll and small-island people thinking in such majestic terms implies a marked degree of mental adaptation. There was nothing small about megalithic thought. Though it could adapt to small sites where necessary, the principal sites in Indonesia are large, demonstrating a rare aesthetic grasp of landscape and panorama.

[1] I am grateful to Tan Sri Haji Abdul Mubin Sheppard for guiding me to the Malayan megaliths which, though in great numbers, are deceptively difficult to locate.

To the Western eye there is something theatrical in megalithic lay-out, which in its essentials is similar to a classical Italian garden that has been designed for open-air theatrical performances.

The Italian garden would have as its rear and focal point a slightly elevated patio backed by a balustrade, which is continued at right angles on either side of the stage. Descending from the entire width of the stage would be three or four stone or marble steps, leading to a wider forestage, the balustrade running out from both sides of the steps, then once again coming down at right angles to two points making downstage right and left, on each of which there would probably be an urn on a pedestal. This basic pattern of rectangles of diminishing size, each with an open front, narrowing to a raised focal point in the centre, is the typical megalithic formation, the right-angle points of each rectangle being marked by a pile or some simple edifice.

Approaching the formation, dead in line with the central focal point, and preferably on an ascending slope, are usually two edifices, occupying the positions which in the operatic theatre are taken by the *régisseur* and the conductor of the orchestra.

Ideally such a formation was built into the side of a mountain, the focal point being on a protuberance, or bluff, if there was one, with two arms of the mountain falling on either side of it. This is a selection similar to that of the geomantic siting of Chinese tombs, save for the fact that what the eye sees in terms of geographical features when looking straight out from the central focal point is not important, which in Chinese geomancy it is.

The megalithic formation faced the population area it was designed to protect in a religious sense. The atoll religion being ancestral, whatever religious ideas may have been connected with megalithic construction in its land of origin, in Indonesia the religious idea involved was ancestral. From these elevated platforms, majestically sited and embellished with outflanking formations, the ancestors looked down benevolently on their descendants in the land that lay before them.

A typical megalithic monument did not contain any temple buildings, the focal point being frequently empty, it would seem.

The ancestors, always thought of as invisible, had no need of such dwellings.

A fine example of a megalithic monument still in use, having been adapted to Hinduism, is to be seen in Bali at Besákih, the 'Mother Temple' of the Balinese people. Besákih stands well up on the slopes of Gunong Agung, Bali's highest and most impressive volcano. Sited on a protuberance, it faces south-west, the direction of the island's main centre of population, which it surveys distantly, and guards. With the ribs of the mountain descending outward on either side, the entire conception is that of the mountain itself, symbolizing the mother of mankind, standing facing her people with arms extended.

It is possible that Besákih, as tradition states, has been Hindu since its foundation in the second century A.D. If this is so, then it was designed on megalithic principles. It appears, however, to be a megalithic monument of great antiquity, adapted later to Hinduism.

In the siting of megalithic monuments there is no apparent connexion with points of the compass or with astronomy. This suggests, firstly, that astronomy had declined in the easier navigating conditions of Asia, and secondly, that the outside influence involved, whatever it was, was not so intimately connected with astronomy as was the Pacific civilization. Both this and the grandeur of megalithic lay-out in relation to large expanses of land indicate a continental origin for this influence.

Apart from the directional relation between monument and population, the remainder of choice was dictated by aesthetic factors, making the megalithic mind in some ways remarkably attractive, their sense of landscape in no way differing from ours.

Effect on dance-drama

In this beginning of formal construction among the atoll-transferred people, an aesthetic pattern was laid which has never really changed. This can be noted by examining what happened to the South Indian schools of dancing, Kathakali and Baratanatyam, when they were brought across to Java during the Brahminical Hindu period.

Baratanatyam, the most evolved of all forms of human expression in dance, was originally temple dancing performed by women. Where it survives in Bali today, as in the *Baris* dance, it still is performed by women, giving incredibly convincing expositions of the inner character of men.

Kathakali, the origins of which could be called more secular, had its traditional place of performance in the open air, often beside a large banyan tree which served as a focal point for a people's gathering.

In either case, whether in a temple court or in the open air, the audience entirely surrounded the performers. It was 'theatre in the round'. As a result, all the dance movements are rotatory. When dancing, one has to remember that at any given moment one has one's back to a quarter of the audience. Rotatory movement in addition symbolized the universe.

To an astonishing degree the spirit and character of these two magnificent dance forms were transferred to Java and Bali. The *mudras*, or gestures, in which every movement of a finger has a definite verbal meaning, were simplified in intellectual content, many of them becoming gestures of emotion, the Indonesian mind finding the intensely literary thought-content of South Indian dancing too intricate for them. In every other respect the transference of idea and technique is complete and perfect, though re-enacted in a far-distant setting, expressing different ideas for a different people.

Every essential was transferred except the fundamental basis – rotatory movement. This ran full-tilt into megalithic ideas of form.

A megalithic monument has, in theatrical terms, a backdrop. This may, as in the case of Besákih, be a 10,000-foot volcano, or it may be just a little mound in horseshoe shape, as at Pengkalan Kempas, in Negri Sembilan. But it is a backdrop; and without it the megalithic monument would never have been designed.

Fundamental to megalithic thought is a background wall, real or imagined, which the people face. In Indonesia the wall signified the beyond (the ancestors), the ensemble being a presentment of the people facing their ancestors, the ancestors facing them, which in constructed outward form was a replica of the inner spiritual form of the atolls.

The depth to which the megalithic concept sank into the soul of the people was occasioned by this being, in visible terms, an explanation of something of profound importance, which on an atoll could only dwell in the spirit, but which had now at long last found symbolic physical expression.

Thus, while the style, spirit and content of South Indian dancing were adopted, the footwork and manner of presentation were altered to conform with megalithic ideas. The subject-matter of Indian dance being sacred, the idea of an audience sitting all round it was unthinkable, having the effect of *excluding* the sacred (the ancestors). Anything sacred required a wall, real or imagined, with the audience on the remaining three sides, the action of the dance being played 'out front'.

Perhaps only those versed in South Indian dance, whether as performer or amateur, will appreciate how extraordinary this is. To such, it is always fascinating to observe this gently adamant cultural refusal to conform to Hindu lay-out, with its circular, non-ancestral view of the universe.

When Indian and Balinese dance forms were first seen in European theatres, it was noticeable how the Indians had problems of adaptation which they seldom succeeded in overcoming, their performers being so often with their backs to the audience. The Balinese, on the other hand, took to the Western stage without difficulty. It was even easier for them, since the entire audience was out front, and they did not have to worry about those on the sides, as would have been necessary in Bali.

It is a strange thought that the reason for this was megalithic.

Music

The same period marks the introduction into Java of a new and non-Pacific form of music.

The modes used in *gamelan* music would seem to have their origin in China as it was, prior to the southward expansion of the Chinese culture, and in the Indo-Chinese peninsula. These modes are *sui generis*, unlike anything else to be found in the music of Asia. In its early evolution this kind of music must have been performed by means of cunningly contrived wooden gongs – as it were, small resonant drums striking each a different note. With the coming of metal casting the style obviously took a great step forward, becoming the percussive gong music of today. It is the modes and the use of contrasting keys, however, which give this music its unique features.

The older Pacific forms of music survived, as they still do, notably in the *Kechak*, the celebrated 'dance' of Hanuman's monkeys in the *Ramayana* story as performed in Bali, in which no musical instrument is used. Apart from this, percussive music of the megalithic period triumphed. When later on stringed instruments and woodwind were introduced from India, they made only limited headway wherever they encountered *gamelan* music, while Indian musical theory, scales, modes (*ragas*) and forms of expression made no impression, except in remote places such as Flores, and on the small island of Roti, off the south-western tip of Timor, in both of which places string instruments based on Indian theories of design became popular.

This illustrates the deep formative impression made on Indonesian thought during this period. A Pacific people, very musical and with refined religious ideas, but with a background acutely sparse in material things – the atoll – made their first encounter with a continental influence with ideas and the wherewithal to give new and richer expression to religion, music and the arts. The experience made a profound impression on them, laying a cultural foundation which has never been touched. Everything that happened afterwards in the main current of artistic development in Java and Bali is an embellishment resting on this megalithic foundation, made of materials which the ancestors lacked.

15 Irrigation and Old Hinduism

circa 800–240 B.C.

Still in the period of the megaliths, around 800 B.C., the science of irrigation, wet cultivation of rice, and the domesticated buffalo were introduced into Java from India.

The activity of an influential intermediary is discernible in this, a person of intelligence familiar both with India and Indonesia – either the foreign financial adviser to a prospering Javanese community, or one of the continental traders dealing with him. Also discernible is an Indonesian ruler who was an innovator with considerable resources.

Java, grassy and gaunter in appearance than it is today, due to rainwater everywhere running unchecked to the sea, had the highest of what were nowhere large populations. On atolls the Austronesian breeding capacity had seemed prodigious; in a more landed environment it was less spectacular. All in the region, except Melanesians and one or two remote inland tribes, were rice-eaters, burning and shifting within individual community and chieftainly areas.

Ceremonial trade had dwindled away, eroded first by its imperceptible shift to barter trade, and dealt a critical blow when various types of pre-metal money – cowrie shells, etc. – came to be used as a medium of exchange along Asia's continental coasts. Except among a few inveterates, the voyaging instinct had lessened. What remained of Austronesia in Asia had become landed communities, though ever with a house on stilts and a boat underneath it, in case the river flooded or there was an exceptionally high tide.

As the centuries passed, and continental activity (alien, resourceful and resented) became more pronounced in the waters of Southern Asia, many of those on the fringes of the region, unaffected by megalithic influence and holding strongly to old traditions, became disillusioned with conditions. In the mid-sixth century B.C. there was an influx of northern Indians into Ceylon, causing numbers of

Austronesian-speaking people on that island – the population segment which had not intermarried with local people – to sail west to join their distant brethren in Madagascar. In the following century, others in the Moluccas returned to the atolls and islands of the Pacific, to become the masters of Micronesia.[1]

In one way it was a crumbling world. Yet for some it was not. In the conviction and self-confidence given to the landbased by megalithic influence, a significant number had at last crossed the difficult threshold between a civilization of ocean and a civilization of earth.

The introduction of irrigation was a considerable operation, demanding careful organization, the use of international trade facilities, and the resources and manpower at the disposal of a prosperous ruler. It was not simply a matter of bringing new strains of seed and explaining the principles of irrigation. Men had to be brought who were skilled agriculturalists with an understanding of water utilization, together with labourers to build the first works, demonstrate the first and second planting, and teach the regulation of water in relation to growing rice.

Nor could this have been done on the basis of one visit. Irrigation in its early phases is a matter of trial and error, due to the unexpected things that happen whenever water is diverted from its natural flow. Many years of trial and error lie behind all the older irrigation works in Asia, demanding the presence of experts and the support of chieftainly organization.

In addition, men were required to look after buffaloes. The buffalo is a temperamental and sensitive creature, who becomes ungovernable if not handled by someone who understands him, and with whom he feels an affinity. To have transported buffaloes to Indonesia without their skilled handlers would have been out of the question.

Though in relation to the total population of Java the degree of Hindu settlement was small, quite a number of men were needed, even for the first and earliest irrigation projects. As the idea caught on, and neighbouring communities in other parts of the island

[1] See Chap. 11, *infra.*

decided they too wanted to go in for it, more experts and labourers from India were required, together with more buffaloes and men to handle them, until the animal established itself by local breeding, and Indonesians learned how to handle him, by developing that quality of human response without which no buffalo will work.

Where ocean traders and travellers were concerned – and it is plainly from one of them that the idea came to introduce irrigation in Java – the first place in India where irrigation was to be seen was Kérala, the extreme south-western part of the Malabar coast, formerly the states of Travancore and Cochin.

There, with pullulating vegetation and abundant water, irrigation could be seen close to ports and coasts. Kérala, one of India's oldest trading centres, lay on the main route of trade between the Persian Gulf and the Far East. It was probably from someone's experience of Kérala that the idea was born.

The actual operations, however, were organized from Bengal, a riverine but similarly pullulating area, where irrigation was to be found close to trading settlements.

Due to the need to feed and water them, buffaloes could not be transported on the month-long voyage from Ceylon to Sumatra, nor was it practicable to water them along the difficult Coromandel coast. From Bengal, by hugging the eastern coasts of the Bay at the favourable season it was possible, with much difficulty and making slow progress, to make it to the Strait of Malacca, coasting thence through the islands and along the eastern shores of Sumatra – where irrigation belongs to the same early period – to reach Java.

In Bengal, too, were to be found craft suitable for transporting buffaloes. The lower reaches of the Ganges have since ancient times been noted for large-scale riverine boatbuilding. The largest and strongest of these vessels were those used as cargo-carriers in the Sundarbans – the Beautiful Forests – which fringe the mouths of the Ganges.

Consisting more of forest and less of jungle than they later became, the Sundarbans were a scene of much human activity, where all transport was by boat; and boats had to be strong enough to weather open-sea conditions. In wide cargo-carriers, of shallow draught but sturdy, the first buffaloes travelled to Sumatra and Java from this region.[1]

Though such vessels could be sailed, on these voyages they were more probably towed by large and strongly manned Indonesian paddled canoes. Additional swift vessels would have been required to go ahead to lay in fodder and water from along the coasts, to be brought out to the dumb craft, shortening the journey time by rendering it unnecessary for the animals to be brought ashore except where conditions were specially favourable, i.e. where landing was easy and there were reliable contacts ashore.

All told, each of these voyages was a major undertaking and a remarkable achievement. This was evidently how it was done, giving rise to an age-old belief, still held in some of the riverine villages near the Sundarbans, that Hinduism reached Java from Bengal – as indeed, in the shape of field labourers and buffalo handlers, it did.

Those who left their homes in India and travelled south into the unknown were humble people, recruited and hired by some unknown but enlightened Indonesian treasurer-chieftain, using foreign traders as his agents. All who came from India on these journeys were of low caste. The handling of buffaloes is a low-caste occupation in India, as is field labour; and these were the men who were needed. No Brahmin or member of the higher castes, even had they been required, would in any case have consented to come, to leave the shores of India being to lose caste.[2] Those who came, being of the Sudra, the lowest of the four main castes, had nothing much to lose in this respect.

In Indonesia they found themselves in the two-caste society of

[1] For an account of this identical voyage, made in the second century B.C., see Appendix 4.

[2] It is sometimes maintained in India that the caste prohibition on leaving the motherland is not as old as this. There is no evidence to support such a contention. The people of Tamil Nad, the largest and most prominent of the civilizations of South India, were markedly cosmopolitan, and the region has had international trade connexions as far back as trade can be traced; but there is no suggestion that prominent people ever went abroad. Others came to them, as was also the case with the Malayalam civilization of the Malabar coast.

Insular Asia. Caste coming as no surprise to them, they themselves
fitted into this caste system, joining the rest who were the *ata*, or
lower caste.

The principal points of contact with India were Kérala and
Bengal. As report spread in these two places of faraway islands where
conditions of life for the lowly were incomparably better than anything to be found by such people in India, a vogue for emigration
set in. Malabaris from Kérala, by one pretext or another, managed to
obtain passage in eastward-bound trading ships, while others came
south from Bengal.

Such men did not fare so well as those who had been recruited and
hired. A number of them eventually settled in the archipelago eastward of Bali. There, being unsubsidized, they developed no irrigation, adapting themselves, as had the Pacific people before them, to
shifting cultivation of hill rice.[1]

Owing to increasing trade movement in Eastern seas, even after
demand for expert labour in Indonesia ceased, here and there a
migrant or two managed to arrive from Kérala and Bengal, their
movement aided by the demand for spices in Egypt and, as metal
came ever more into general use, by the discovery and exploitation of
minerals in South-East Asia.

In Indonesia, under these slow and gentle influences, Hindu
ideas spread and entrenched themselves. The Overseas Indians,
though poor and needy, were in some ways superior to the local
people. Their more advanced skills were needed and appreciated,
and they understood regular labour, something which lay entirely
outside Insular Asia's experience. With irrigation on a non-seasonal
basis, time became related to work, demanding an important
adjustment of mind and habit. This had to be taught – by Indians.

This being the position, when Indians spoke of their religious
ideas, of which, then as now, the lower castes had a refined knowledge, local people listened.

---

[1] The Malabari element left its racial imprint mainly in western Flores, the
Bengali element further east on that island, and in Timor. Some of the songs heard
in the Sunday market at Dili, capital of Portuguese Timor, are in pure Bengali
musical idiom, unlike anything else in South-East Asia.

The ancient Melanesians, having nothing supernatural in their ideas, had no gods. Neither had the people of the transferred atoll, for whom there were solely the Creator and ancestors, none of them visible.

More or less everyone had an ancestral animal in the pre-Austronesian world, and in various places, including Java and Bali, these were either associated with, or had become, the gods of the earth, the navel gods, who were local and in their way ancestral.

Thus, in the religious ideas of the time, there was the duality of the invisible ancestors, related to megalithic sites, and the gods of the *pusat*, or navel, of whom statues were made in wicker coated with beaten bark, and painted. Into the invisible department of this duality some of the Hindu gods entered, as described by buffalo handlers and others.

There being no sculptures of these gods, they were invisible entities, like the ancestors – a feature which aided their acceptance by the transferred atoll.

Semángat – the Indonesian name for *mana* – relating the psychic and intangible to material life, was quickly understood by Indians. It was Shakti, the feminine *élan vital* of the universe, who is pure spirit and exists in everything, whether animate or inanimate.

At the beginning of all things in Hinduism stand Purusha and Prakriti, the former eternally motionless and male, the latter female. Creation began when Prakriti moved and spoke, the force created by her movement and speech being Shakti, which invests all that is, and is female.

Apart from the fact that Shakti is female, whereas things powerful in *semángat*, or *mana*, are handled by men, the two concepts are remarkably similar. The only other difference between them is that one is simplistic, deriving from the oldest traceable period of human thought (the Melanesians), while the other, belonging to a later phase in the development of human thought, is a fully embodied philosophic concept.

This is another point at which the people of the transferred atoll encountered from another civilization a concept similar to an idea of their own, which was thereby sustained. *Semángat* was strengthened in the mind of the people by its encounter with Shakti.

In fact, though neither side realized this, there was a difference of approach, which among humble Indians of the kind who came to Indonesia would have been less discernible than among educated Hindus of the higher castes.

Hinduism, in all its varied forms, is a working hypothesis, containing nothing resembling belief or faith as these words are understood in the West. A Hindu does not believe in Shakti; he postulates her as a hypothetical likelihood. In Indonesia there was a different mental approach. There was complete conviction in things, such as is not found in Hindu thought.

Indonesians did not believe in *semángat* any more than Indians believed in Shakti. Indonesians regarded *semángat* as an established fact of existence, similar to the sun and moon. When they performed any action relating to *semángat*, they did so with complete conviction of that action's necessity (magic). This element of conviction in their thinking was in due course to give Indonesian Hinduism its special character, of which the main features are that it was ancestral Hinduism, unlike anything to be found in India, and contained nothing hypothetical.

In the same way as *semángat* was sustained by its meeting with Shakti, so was Indonesian caste in its meeting with Hindu caste. From what Indonesians learned of the latter, the two caste systems seemed to be alike. In fact, they were different. The Hindu castes indicated divisions of human activity: intellectual, civil and military, commercial and manual. The Indonesian castes represented *au fond* a plain distinction between rulers and ruled. Because the two appeared to be the same, caste in Indonesia was strengthened.

During this period the Indonesian castes acquired names, given them by Indian settlers, and which became general. In Flores and Timor these caste names survive to this day, as do the castes themselves. Though these two islands are largely Christian, this has had no effect on caste. All Christian marriages are made in conformity with the caste divisions, no inter-caste marriage being socially acceptable.

The caste names which will be used here are those of Portuguese Timor, which are the most representative of those that have survived, not having been tampered with by later influences. The upper caste is called *liu rai*, meaning 'descended from kings', while the lower caste, representing the bulk of the population, are called *ata*, usually translated as 'slaves', or *ata-wan*, 'slave people'.[1]

As the earlier description of the *ata* in the *barangay* will have made clear, the word does not mean 'slaves' in the Western sense. The *ata* could own property, and though they were in a sense owned jointly by the upper caste, they were also that caste's responsibility. Above all, there is the difference that to be owned was an advantage, not a disadvantage. Not to be owned was to be an outlaw.

Moreover, it was of special advantage, within the general framework of this relationship of ownership and responsibility, to be immediately owned by, or particularly associated with, an influential or prominent member of the upper caste, or be one of a group of such. Men of the *ata* could shift their personal allegiances, and they aimed to do this to their own advantage, lessening their ties with an ageing or dwindling *liu rai*, joining a prominent or up-and-coming one – which in early times usually meant someone notable as a warrior.

Reverting to the Sri Vijaya fleets mentioned in an earlier chapter, the nature of the relationship between the commander and 'his' men becomes more distinct. In addition to the commander, there were in each of the fleet's vessels one or two men of the same social status or caste, as himself, between whose families marriage was possible. Each would have 'his' men, the most fortunate of these, in their own estimation, being those who were the commander's men, standing in direct owner-responsibility relation to him.

The real difference between the two castes concerns responsibility and decision-making. Throughout mankind in this region, decision-

---

[1] The provenance of the word *liu rai* is Bengal. *Ata* is the root word for the lower of the two castes which in ancient times were to be found across the whole of Southern Asia. The Philippine word *tao*, which has come to mean the rustic common man, is a shortened version of *ata-o*, meaning 'slave people'. In Indonesia and Malaysia the word used is *rakyat*, which has come to mean the common people. *Rakyat* is a Persian word meaning 'chattels'; applied to human beings it has the same connotation as *ata* translated as 'slaves', being in fact a Persian version of the same root word. The Japanese word *eta*, meaning 'unclean people', and applied to despised castes pursuing objectionable trades, derives from the same source.

7. Prambánan, Central Java:
'. . . perhaps the most beautiful
of all Hindu monuments. . . .'

Prambánan: four-headed
Brahma. Hindu statues in
Indonesia are portraits of
people who actually lived –
in marked contrast with
India.

8. Ancestral tradition in Bali.
Left: '. . . while demons and monstrosities are sculpted, the gods are not.'
Below: A Balinese split gate, indicating the invisible presence of the ancestors.

making and the exercise of responsibility have been confined since time immemorial to the small *liu rai* caste, in relation to whom the *ata* have been persons of diminished responsibility. Moreover, what was advantageous to them in being one of 'his' men to a prominent *liu rai* was not that it increased their responsibility, but that it had the effect of lessening it still further. With an ageing or dwindling *liu rai* a certain element of responsibility might be called for, with an influential or prominent one, none.

The effect produced by the perpetuation of these castes was to inculcate among the *ata* a mentality in which the less responsibility a man had, the more fortunate he considered himself to be; and this has come through to the present age, wherever people of the transferred atoll are to be found.

After *liu rai* and *ata* were formalized by receiving names, a further formalization followed. The upper caste divided into two: a royal caste, and a ministerial or administrative (or military officer) caste. This development is so typical of Hindu thought as to make its source transparent. These two castes clearly began as typically analytical Indian definitions, into which they hardened with time, till throughout the greater part of atoll-transferred Indonesia – i.e. not among tribal people – there were three castes.

Timor escaped this. In Flores the three-caste structure is still to be found: the *Ria-béwa*, the royal or princely caste; the *Mosa-laki*, the caste from which the rulers of Hindu times drew their civil and military officers; and (the bulk of the population) the *Ata ko-o*, or slave people.

Thus between the eighth and third centuries B.C., Indonesia became a Hindu region – of a kind. The Philippines were also touched by Hinduism, though not to the same extent. In Ceylon, where irrigation and unlettered Hinduism are older than in Indonesia, a similar caste pattern formed, with the upper rice-measuring class becoming the highest caste, a place which, as landed gentry, they have maintained ever since.

In Indonesia there were Hindu gods (unsculpted) in addition to the ancestors, a three-tier caste system, cremation, an absolute prohibition on the slaughter of cows, and many Hindu stories and legends.

Having been introduced by the uneducated and illiterate, as Hinduism it was far from complete. The Indian immigrants were not teachers, and there were no Brahmins. At the top of the Indonesian caste structure were those who in India would have been members of the second caste, the Kshattriya. The topmost caste, the Brahmin – teacher and intellectual – was missing.

While stories and legends came, and gods came, the philosophic content of which they are expressions was limited. It was precisely this – Hinduism introduced with a low content of philosophy – which enabled the Hindu world to expand as it did.

This form of Hinduism – without Brahmins, philosophy, literature, temples, or plastic arts – endured till towards the end of the third century B.C. It can be referred to, in its Indonesian context, as Old Hinduism.

It embraced the entire archipelago, from Sumatra to Timor. It penetrated Borneo, where certain of its features – cremation, prohibition on killing deer, and numerous stories – were still just discernible as past memories when the history of that island first came to be written. It embraced the southern part of Celebes, where it had the same effect as in Java of strengthening and confirming the caste divisions of society. It was reaching out to the Moluccas by 450 B.C. or thereabouts, when Austronesians in those islands – including the Gilbertese – began their epic return journey to the atolls of the Pacific.

Lacking teachers and intellectuals, Old Hinduism accommodated far more than would have been acceptable in India. Cannibalism among the Batak of Sumatra, human sacrifice on Flores, psychic communication with the ancestors, propitiation of the gods of the navel, magic, these and many other religious features coexisted with it. Old Hinduism was a disordered *mélange* of Hindu and non-Hindu ideas and practice, part of the long process of cultural accretion which is the story of Indonesia, in particular of its centres of civilization, Java and Bali.

There remains the mystery of the most spectacular of all Asia's irrigation works, the rice terraces of the Mountain Province in Luzon. In that these seem to date from the period of Old Hinduism, it is possible that they are an outcome of influence from Indonesia, while it would certainly seem to be from Indonesia that irrigation and the buffalo reached the Philippines, along the link of related languages and culture, with Indonesians, not Indians, showing how to construct the first works, double-plant the rice, and regulate the water.

The people of the Minahassa, in North Celebes, are close kin of the Filipinos of northern Luzon, and being an adventurous people with wide seafaring contacts, it could well be they who were responsible for this development.

The Ifugao and Igorot people have similar stories concerning the semi-divine origin of their rice terraces. In the Bontóc region of the Mountain Province these are ascribed to Lumáwig, a being who descended from the sky, married a local girl, and taught agriculture. Yet somehow the mind boggles at such matchless ingenuity developing among peoples living in isolation. Invention and development spring from the encounter of different cultures; in isolation humans remain with what they have, or deteriorate.

16 Brahminical Hinduism in Indonesia

Third century B.C. to fifteenth century A.D.

In Indian history there is one special moment which could have prompted men of high caste to take the drastic and irrevocable step of leaving the country, thereby losing caste. This was during the second part of the reign of the Emperor Ashoka (274–232 B.C.), when Buddhism, hitherto a minor non-conformist Hindu sect, was imposed on India as the national religion, the privileged position of the Brahmins being no longer recognized at the imperial court.

Western historians, in their enthusiasm for Ashoka, the first ruler to unite the Indian subcontinent, have generally failed to grasp the implications of the fact that Buddhism was imposed on India. The high-minded sentiments expressed by the emperor in stone on the Ashoka pillars and other relics betoken a monarch of enlightenment and humanity, and have won today's admiration. In fact, at the time, many an educated Hindu of the higher castes would have regarded those engraved words with cynicism.

We of today see only how a powerful monarch, having subdued India in one gory battle after another, underwent an exalted change of mind, refrained from making his final conquest in the South, and from then on enjoined non-violence and obedience to the Buddhist scriptures. What is more difficult to perceive is that, to many an educated Indian of those times, Ashoka's noble sentiments wore an air of sectarian bigotry.

Ashoka ranks as a convert to Buddhism. Like many converts, he held unusually strong views about the altered course he had taken. Buddhism being the emperor's course, all must follow it; and he went to great lengths to see they did. Even the men of his armed forces had to spend much of their day listening to Buddhist sermons instead of doing military exercises.

The Buddha having advocated an egalitarian, casteless society,

Ashoka no longer recognized the caste divisions, with the predictable result that many Brahmins and men of high worth – Brahmins performed numerous important civic functions, as well as religious – discreetly put distance between themselves and authority, while at court many wily *parvenus* from lower castes, with elaborate display of Buddhist righteousness and murmuring of sutras, were able to attain positions to which their birth did not entitle them, with duties for which doubtless some of them had little aptitude. The balance of an old and powerful society was disturbed.

This is the one moment in Indian history which could have prompted Brahmins, and others of high caste, to quit India. Ashoka, for all his new-found pacifism, was extremely powerful, the mightiest monarch India had ever known. It would have been difficult for a prominent man to elude the imperial insistence on Buddhist conformity.

Only in the extreme south was there an unconquered region where such a man could be out of the emperor's reach. This was precisely one of the regions enjoying contacts with Indonesia. On the Malabar coast, and generally throughout the South, it was known that somewhere way to the east was a fully Hindu island – a piece of information which for a Brahmin could have mitigated the blow of leaving the shores of his land.

In Bengal, particularly in the lower reaches of the Ganges delta, similar information was available concerning Java; and the Sundarbans, with their special connexion with Java, have throughout Indian history figured as a hiding place where prominent persons out of favour could enjoy immunity from authority.

It is to this period, therefore, that the coming of Brahmins and handwriting to Java attaches itself, from the same two places – Kérala and Bengal. The seat of empire being in the north, Bengal was probably the more important of the two escape routes.[1]

The Maurya dynasty, of which Ashoka was the outstanding figure, was succeeded after a relatively short lapse of time by the Kushan period, the empire of the White Huns, under which Buddhism was protected and flourished for a few centuries. Again,

[1] See Appendix 7: Agastya.

it was a time when an orthodox Hindu of high caste, under heavy personal pressure, might have contemplated leaving India for lands overseas, in what was gradually becoming Further India.

Later, around the first century A.D., trade developed between South-East Asia and ports on the Coromandel coast. These South Indian kingdoms being Hindu, it is unlikely that anyone of high caste went abroad.[1]

Those who came to Indonesia assumed a Brahminical position at the head of society. Had the fabric of Old Hinduism not existed, they could not have taken this position except in conditions of an Indian invasion and occupation, of which there is no trace. The fact is that by the third century B.C., in the more populous and civilized islands of Indonesia, the structure of a Hindu society existed, into which the one missing element, the Brahmins, fitted without difficulty. It being known that they were a missing element, they were doubtless welcomed. This is doubly understandable when reflecting that they gave the major Indonesian languages their first scripts.

The number of Brahmins who came from India was not high, nor did they expand into the horde of literate drones which they became in many parts of India. Upper-caste society in Indonesia remained predominantly Kshattriya, the second caste. Brahmins only settled in areas of high culture – or, to put it another way, their numbers being few, the high culture which their arrival stimulated only occurred in certain areas; it was not general.

Those areas were Java, parts of southern Sumatra, and Bali. Elsewhere there is little sign of them. In more remote islands, such as Flores and Timor, the pattern of society remained that of Old Hinduism. There is no Brahmin caste on any of these islands, nor any suggestion that there has ever been one.

Whether Brahmins established themselves in the Philippines is doubtful. If they did, it would have been as men of learning, not as priest-teachers. While Hindu ideas and stories penetrated the Philippines, the fabric of Old Hinduism – dependent as it was on

[1] From this time onward, however, Indonesia's principal contacts were with South India, and lower caste people undoubtedly went abroad.

Indians – did not exist there. The caste structure of Old Hinduism being lacking, a Brahmin could not, as in Indonesia, take a pre-eminent position in society. He would have been treated simply as a learned kind of landless *datu*. Since the first scripts of the Philippine languages are Sanskritic, it is quite possible that Brahmins were responsible for this, though with the foregoing modification as regards their social status.

Such Philippine Hindu works of art as survived the rigorous suppression of pre-Christian culture conducted by the Spanish friars convey a rustic impression, suggestive of a people who were only on the fringe of things Hindu. They lack the refinement and polish of Javanese works of art. Unfortunately for the investigator, the most commonly used material for Hindu works of art in the Philippines was gold – virtually every man, woman and child in the islands wore gold ornaments – and no work of art vanishes faster than a gold one.[1]

During the epoch of Further India, the Philippines received their principal Hindu influences along the link of related language, from Indonesia, and from Champa (south-east Vietnam), where the principal language was an Austronesian one.[2]

Whereas Indonesia, with direct contact with India, responded to Hindu influence by evolving some of the world's most impressive art forms, the Philippines, where contacts with India were indirect, did not. Against this must be set the fact that the principal continental immigrants in the islands were Chinese, indifferent to Hindu ideas and culture, and providing them with neither moral nor monetary support.

What the Spanish friars eventually found was an extraordinary amalgam of ancestral ideas, small gods (similar to the gods of the navel), magic, ancestral animals, psychic communicants, Hindu-style

[1] Even since 1950, when I first knew the Philippines, evidence of the Hindu period has diminished – presumably melted down. The principal cult, as throughout most of Further India, was Saivite; and there was an influential Tantric element, derived presumably from the Indo-Chinese peninsula, there being no evidence that Tantra, either in Hindu or Buddhist guise, ever made any lasting impression in Indonesia.

[2] Though it may not have been the language of the Court.

stories and poetry, Hindu symbology, Hindu scripts which were at the time giving way to newly introduced Arabic, Tantra, and an atoll social formation which had divided itself into the two pre-Austronesian castes.

Upon this amalgam, in which no single element was particularly strong except the castes, which were undetected, the friars imposed Christianity. In the process, which was thorough, a different man came into being, between whom and his past there is a cultural rift.

The same happened in Ceylon with the advent of Buddhism. The arrival of large numbers of northern Indians in the sixth century B.C. merely led to an adjustment of existing conditions, which were probably not dissimilar to Old Hinduism. Buddhism, arriving three centuries later, placed a rift between a Singhalese and his past, much of which, as in the Philippines, went 'underground'. It is there to this day, though hard to detect, still harder to explain.

Only in Indonesia, where there was no cultural assault, where the Austronesian ship sailed smoothly on without a collision, can the story of the Pacific people be brought coherently to the point where it encounters history.

The Brahmins in Indonesia found themselves in a position resembling that of the Christian missionaries of the nineteenth century.[1] Being thin on the ground, they realized it was useless to think of introducing Sanskritic language. If they were to teach Hindu philosophy, which they would have regarded as urgently needed in the conditions of Old Hinduism, with its low content of philosophy, their first occupation must be to learn local languages and reduce them to handwriting. In this they encountered the stumbling block which from that day to this has prevented the diffusion of philosophic or any deep intellectual thought, wherever Austronesian languages are spoken.

In the transference from the Melanesian Age to the Austronesian, what was witnessed was the move of the human mind from the local to the universal, by means of a language in which universal ideas can be expressed. The development of Hindu thought repre-

[1] Tradition in Bengal indicates that there was a missionary spirit among those who left the country.

sents another such movement of the human mind: from the universal to the analysis of it, again in relation to a language – Sanskrit – welded to analytical thought, as supremely embodied in Hindu philosophy. The human mind moved into an age of analysis.

Thought of this kind, belonging to a more advanced stage of man's mental development, cannot be expressed in an Austronesian language. These languages belong to a period before man thought in so analytical a manner. Not only are the terms of analysis absent in such languages: their syntax is resistant to the exactitudes of thought which analysis demands.

This difficulty is the same today as it was then. The most evolved of contemporary Austronesian-derived languages is Tagálog, the principal local language of the Philippines. To take a paragraph from a Sanskrit classic and translate it into Tagálog, it would first be necessary to reorganize the thought formation of each segment of the paragraph, splitting it into small separate sentences, using Sanskrit words for key terms. Even then, it would be found that the final Tagálog rendering was a simplified and inexact version of the original, really only understandable to someone with a knowledge of Sanskrit, who, by mentally re-translating it into that tongue, might possibly be able to discern what it meant.

This was the difficulty the Brahmins encountered in spreading comprehension of Hindu philosophy. It is also, parenthetically, the reason why the *mudras* in Baratanatyam became gestures of emotion when transferred to Bali. The literary thought behind the *mudras* was untranslatable in an Indonesian language.

Thus, while educated Indians had a notable influence on the arts, and in the spread of the written word, the period of Brahminical Hinduism is notable for its absence of philosophy. Such Hindu philosophy as reached Indonesia spread only among a select few in courtly circles, where alone it could be understood and appreciated. The mass of the people were unaffected by it.

Indeed, had Brahmins and educated Indians been the first to reach Indonesia, Hinduism would probably have made no impact whatever. Coming as it did through the medium of the humble and illiterate, it was purveyed in the form of stories. This being a form of transmission ideally suited to Austronesian language, Hindu ideas took root.

At some stage the Hindu epics, the *Ramayana* and the *Mahabharata*, reached Java.[1] These, being in story form, made a profound impression, becoming so popular, so much part of the people, that not even Islam, which destroyed much in its path, was able to dislodge them, the Hindu epics being to this day the inspirational fountainhead of the arts in Java and Bali, and the people's favourite stories.

Apart from this, the feature of Brahminical Hinduism which had the deepest effect on Java was mysticism. Being largely wordless, mysticism did not encounter the same linguistic obstacle as did philosophy.

Psychic communication with the ancestors was a feature of religious practice which the atoll people had brought with them from the Pacific. This met and blended with the intellectually more advanced mysticism of India – another of those meetings of similar though actually unrelated ideas which had a sustaining and strengthening effect on atoll influences. These at a later date encountered Islamic mysticism, which still further sustained them into the present age.

Whereas in India, owing to the eternal struggle for existence demanded by poor soil and frequent failure of rains, a mystic has a struggle to pursue his course, in Java's boundless natural richness, with an ease of living almost unparalleled, mysticism found more devotees than would have been possible in India. There being less struggle in life, there was more time for it. With it came Hindu ideas of abstinence and withdrawal, of cleaving *away* from material things. This in turn had an indirect effect on perpetuating the absence of understanding of the time–money relationship.

It has rightly been said that every Javanese is at heart a mystic.

---

[1] During the period of Old Hinduism, and *before* the epics came to be set down in writing in India. The versions of the epics known in Indonesia today show many signs of being older than the current versions in India. In fact, the student of the epics needs to give serious attention to the Indonesian versions, which clearly give clues to the oral originals from which Valmiki and others worked.

In this his Pacific soul responded to nourishment from continental influences, first Hindu, later Islamic.

Finally, with Brahminical Hinduism came the evolution of the king.

Kings in India were essentially military, though with Brahmin aid they sought to endow themselves with divine grace. In Indonesia, when treasurer-chieftains expanded into kings, the religious aspect took on a new tone, arising from that quality of conviction noted earlier, which is not to be found in Indian thought.

In this mental environment, if the king was endowed with divine grace, then he embodied it. From this train of thought arose the king who was a divine emanation, usually of Vishnu or Siva, though later also of accreted Hindu-Buddhist Boddhisattvas. Also, of course, the religion of the transferred atoll being ancestral, the king became the supreme communicant with ancestors.

This last was a highly unusual feature for a Hindu monarch. Due to the theory of reincarnation, ancestors have never played much part in Hinduism. One's own son, after all, might be one of one's ancestors reincarnate. Brahminical Hinduism in Indonesia, faced with conviction in respect of ancestors, found itself obliged to adapt to this or wither away. This culture of accretion, receptive to what is new, yet preserved certain characteristics on which it was unyielding.

To such an extent was Brahminical Hinduism confined to courts that many have doubted whether the Hindu caste system ever obtained in Java. The *Nágara-kertágama* of Prapancha, written around A.D. 1365, makes it plain beyond dispute that the four castes of orthodox Hinduism – Brahmin, Kshattriya, Vaisya and Sudra – existed and were recognized, with the same particular feature as in India that the priestly caste ranked superior to kings, who belonged to the second caste.

These castes, however, were imposed over the already existing castes of Old Hinduism, which in turn had been imposed on the two original castes – rulers and ruled.

This last distinction was maintained, with no yielding to the occupational nature of Hindu caste. The *ata* – 95% of the population – became the Sudra (manual labourers), regardless of whether they were artisans, farmers, shipmasters or actors.

Trade being the monopoly of kings, and the number of fulltime petty traders being few, the Vaisya caste (merchants) was the smallest of the four, its venue the dreamlike Javanese market. Though some of those who traded therein were classified as Vaisya, with Vaisya surnames, they scarcely amounted to a caste. Finding themselves between, on the one side, the unmarriageable upper castes, and 95% of the population on the other, though classified as Vaisya they were in effect Sudra, being in nine cases out of ten obliged to marry Sudra girls.

Only among the *liu rai* was there any application of the occupational nature of Hindu caste. Among the Kshattriya a remnant of the earlier distinction between royal and ministerial (or military) survived, while Brahmins remained more exclusively priestly than in India.

As ever, intermarriage between *liu rai* was permissible, however.[1] The only absolute caste distinction remained the ancient one between *liu rai* and *ata*.

From the time when castes became formalized with names, this distinction intensified, placing a formal obstacle to any liberalizing movement such as those that occurred in the more informal conditions of tribal people, among whom the two castes had no names.

The people of the transferred atoll being culturally more advanced than others, Hinduism made a deeper impression among them than elsewhere. Where its formalities coincided with existing custom, as in the distinction between *liu rai* and *ata*, these proved specially enduring.

It is for this reason that, at the present time, the numerical balance of the two castes – unrecognized, but completely clear in terms of responsibility and initiative – is more unequal among those of the transferred atoll than it is among tribal people or Melanesians. Hinduism reinforced this extreme inequality.[2]

[1] It is to be suspected, though, that marriage between Brahmin and Kshattriya, albeit permitted, was rare. Brahmin children were brought up in a different way, which would have made marriage to a Kshattriya difficult.

[2] See Appendix 4: Hinduism in Indonesia.

17 Into History

Buddhism in Indonesia

Where Brahminical Hinduism made little impression on the Indonesian general population, Buddhism made still less. Buddhism differs from Hinduism in being more institutional, with monasteries and centres of learning, and a form of organized church.

Three different kinds of Buddhism are detectable in Indonesia – atheistic, deistic and popular.

Ashoka's missionary endeavours led to the establishment of an important Buddhist centre in Ceylon. This was Buddhism in its original atheistic form. In Ceylon it preserved a strong missionary spirit, eventually influencing much of the Indo-Chinese peninsula. A centre of this form of Buddhism was established in southern Sumatra in the second century A.D.

Encountering the same linguistic difficulty as had Brahminical Hinduism, it made no impression on local people so far as philosophy was concerned. Being monkish, it was of no appeal to Indonesians as a religion to be actively associated with. Though respected, visited by numerous foreigners, it remained erudite and aloof.

In India, the fourth century A.D. marked the rise of the Gupta empire in the Ganges valley, and with it the Hindu revival. Caste was once more officially recognized, creating another of those moments when dedicated men – this time Buddhists – sought asylum abroad, availing themselves of what were by this time well-established trade routes with reasonably comfortable ships.

This second form of Buddhism, as a result of centuries of exposure to Hinduism, was elaborately deistic. It established important centres in southern Sumatra, later in Java. It was sufficiently imbued with Hindu concepts and deistic stories to give it slightly more local appeal, causing it to obtain an honoured place in royal courts, where it made a significant contribution to the evolution of the king as a divine emanation and supreme communicant with ancestors.

It entirely displaced atheistic Buddhism in Sumatra, where its establishments became world centres of Buddhist learning, of special interest to travellers from China, where deistic Buddhism was favoured, the atheistic form having made no headway in that country.

Buddhism was able to obtain a foothold in Indonesia because it was organized and wealthy. In the forms in which it reached South-East Asia, Buddhism was a religion of the royal and the rich.

In the Indo-Chinese peninsula, with low populations and much land, society was markedly egalitarian. Buddhism of this kind, promoted by missionary geniuses such as Shin Arahan, of the eleventh century in Burma, could in such conditions claim universal acceptance. In Indonesia, locked in the ancient caste system, it made no such appeal.

Remaining exclusively courtly, this second form of Buddhism to arrive in Indonesia achieved a synthesis not only with the first, but with Pacific ancestral religion and megalithic ideas, finally to produce the accreted masterpiece of Borobudur.[1]

Beside it came elements of popular Buddhism, as it was in India in the fourth century A.D., hopelessly intertwined with Hindu deities and stories. This was the only Buddhism to have any effect on ordinary people in Java. In the end it was absorbed into popular Indonesian Hinduism, which Buddhist propagandists failed to undermine. A fierce ideological struggle took place in Java between

[1] Set in magnificent surroundings, Borobudur is sited according to megalithic principles. Its ten ascending platforms represent the ten stages of human advance to Buddhahood. They also represent ten kings of the Sailendra dynasty, nine of whom are thought to have been buried beneath each of the first nine platforms, the tenth to have been cremated on the topmost one. The carvings in the lower platforms comprise the largest collection of the *Jataka* stories ever sculpted in stone, belonging to deistic (Mahayana) Buddhism. The extreme austerity of the topmost platforms belongs to atheistic (Theravada) Buddhism. Thus, at one and the same moment, this is a megalithic monument, an ancestral shrine, a royal mausoleum, and a Buddhist sermon in stone, embodying both the Mahayana and Theravada doctrines.

the two 'popular' religions. It terminated in an agreement, commemorated in Bali to this day by an annual festival marking the
'marriage' of Hinduism and Buddhism, whereby in fact popular
Buddhism was eliminated.

Hindu–Buddhist architecture and sculpture
The Gupta period in India witnessed the first great moment in
Hindu sculpture. It set a vogue of such proportions as to render
Hinduism ever since inseparable from sculpture. It also fulfilled an
important social purpose. Sculpture, together with the theatre
(dance-drama), to which it is closely related, became the literature
of the illiterate. To this day, the ability of a Hindu peasant to enter
into discussion of philosophy is derived from his knowledge of
sculpture, the signs and symbols in which, once known, are as
detailed and explicit as any philosophic treatise.

This vogue for sculpture, followed by another for religious architecture in stone, was with only a slight delay transmitted from India
to Indonesia, bringing into being a Javanese school of architecture
and sculpture which, between the ninth and twelfth centuries A.D.,
achieved unsurpassed heights of artistic achievement.

No Indians were connected with this. The architects and sculptors
were Indonesians who, using the trade routes, studied and travelled
in India, which for the educated few had become a mother country.

The distinction of their thought is exemplified in the fact that
they borrowed only the spirit of Hindu design. Hindu architecture
in Java differs from that of India in its approach to design and the
use of materials. Where stone in India was used to create an impression of massy weight, Javanese architects were trained to use it to
create a feeling of lightness. An indigenous school with wide
connexions overseas, it reached its apogee in the creation of Prambánan in the ninth century.[1]

[1] The site of the Chandi Loro Jonggrang at Prambánan is an exact square. At its
centre, immediately facing the central shrine, was buried a casket of sheets of gold
and silver. This was the refractory point for the king's communication with ancestors. Unlike India, where the cults of Vishnu and Siva were separate, and the cult of
Brahma died out, at major Indonesian temples all three are represented, the tutelary

Where, in India, sculpture brought religion and philosophy closer to the people, in Java it had the effect of drawing such matters further away from them. The *ata* were scarcely affected by these centuries of splendid creation. They were simply the labour force, as required; and labour was occasionally required on a crippling scale.

The masterpieces of Hindu and Buddhist architecture in Java designate a widening of the rift between *liu rai* and *ata*. Erected at monumental expense, taking several reigns to build, the larger of these edifices, devised for communion between king and ancestors, demonstrate on the part of the *liu rai* a degree of self-absorption in which, in regard to the *ata*, all sense of responsibility had gone. Only ownership remained; and this was not the meaning of the relationship.

As to the religion associated with this unique period of sculpture and architecture, to the *ata* the entire subject was esoteric.

The coming of Islam

At this moment of extreme rift and decadence, brought about by a fashionable overplay of Indianism, Islam came over the horizon.

For the *ata* it held one of those irrational yet compelling promises of a political nature. Caste would be abolished, life for ordinary people much improved.

Such was the low position to which the *ata* had been reduced, however, as a result of *liu rai* conceits, fanned by Hindu and Buddhist ideas, that it was impossible for Islam to reach them, except through the intermediary of rulers and their caste. This took time to achieve.

Arabs originally entered East Asian trade as carriers, in Roman times, running voyages on which the traders they bore numbered an

---

being in the centre. At Prambánan the tutelary is Siva Mahadeva, his shrine surrounded by a Vaishnav frieze, one of the greatest masterpieces of Hindu art. The statue of Siva is a portrait of the founder monarch, while in a cell beside it is the statue of his termagant wife as the goddess Durga, standing on Nandi, Siva's bull (symbolizing her husband, the king), twisting its tail with her right hand. Prambánan is a rich example of the strange things that happened to Hinduism in Java.

occasional Arab, but consisted principally of others, notably Jews.
When the Arabs became Muslim – in the seventh century A.D. – the
scope of these voyages lessened, non-Muslims being unwilling to
travel in Arab vessels. Arab contact in the Orient was thereafter
maintained solely with places where Arabs traded and had settled.
Arab trade and settlement, then as now, was small.

Along the east coast of Sumatra, in obscure places out of reach
of the larger Hindu or Buddhist port-kingdoms, minor rulers, as an
outcome of Arab influence, became Muslim, giving the opportunity
to their *ata* – or *rakyat* – to do likewise. Where rulers were dwindling,
the *rakyat* became Muslim regardless of the ruler's wishes. Adoption
of the new religion was found particularly among atoll-transferred
people – coastal and in touch with trading ports. The tribal interior
remained unaffected. By 1285, when Marco Polo made his return
journey by sea from China to Europe, passing Sumatra, there were a
number of these minor Arab-influenced settlements.

The pace of these developments increased in the following century
after Gujerat, in western India, came under Muslim influence.
Released from the caste prohibition on leaving India, numbers of
Gujerati Muslim traders came east in Arab vessels, soon displacing
Arabs, to become the principal international traders.

These Gujeratis had a closer *rapport* with people in Sumatra,
accustomed as many were to contacts with Indians. In the small
kingdoms of Acheh and Pasai, on the north-western tip of Sumatra,
on the main trade route between the Middle and Far East, around
1320 the first Islamic states achieved commercial importance,
largely under Gujerati auspices.

Some eighty years later Malacca, under Hindu maharajas with
antecedents in southern Sumatra, rose to sudden prominence as a
Chinese naval base. This was the brief and exceptional period associated with the Yung Lo reign in China, when Chinese naval fleets
of tremendous power ranged widely in Eastern waters, even sailing as
far as East Africa.

It was quickly recognized that, for commercial purposes, Malacca,
commanding the narrowest point of the Strait, was infinitely better
placed than Acheh. It in fact held the commercial key to the whole

of South-East Asia – and, in the particular circumstances, the religious one as well. It being a Hindu state, however, Gujerati Muslims were unwilling to have dealings with it. Malacca's commerce was thus unspectacular. Despite attempts made from Acheh to persuade the maharaja to convert to Islam, he paid no attention.

In 1432, while he was visiting the Chinese emperor, a crisis occurred in Peking. The palace eunuchs, who were the chief sponsors and beneficiaries of Chinese naval voyages, were ousted from influence by Confucian traditionalists, who suspended the voyages and sealed China off from the outside world.

No one being allowed to leave China while the crisis lasted, the Malacca maharaja was stranded in Peking for about three years. Being at the heart of events, he was in a position to appreciate their magnitude. He saw that the political change was irreversible. Malacca as a Chinese naval base was doomed; it was essential to go over to commerce.

When at last he succeeded in returning to Malacca, he accepted the long-proffered hand of a Muslim princess of Acheh, and in 1436 embraced Islam.[1] Within weeks, Gujerati traders were settling in Malacca, which rapidly became the most important commercial centre in South-East Asia.

So it was in 1509, when the Portuguese first saw it, and when the region as a whole moves into the epoch of consecutively recorded history.

The Malacca conversion gave a powerful *élan* to the spread of Islam in Sumatra, Java, Celebes and the Moluccas, principally by Gujeratis and at points of commerce. From there and from Borneo it established itself in the southern islands of the Philippines, and would have dominated that archipelago completely, had the arrival of the Spaniards in 1565 not put a stop to its further spread.

Majapahit, last of the southern islands' Hindu empires, found itself landlocked in Central Java, all its ports having converted to Islam. Shifting eastward, it ended at Blámbangan, the easternmost point of Java, facing the ultimate and – as it proved – impregnable refuge, which was Bali.

[1] These details have only recently been brought to light in O. W. Wolters: *The Fall of Srivijaya in Malay History*.

While the destruction wrought in Java by zealots of the new religion was culturally a disaster, it is difficult, in terms of the *rakyat*,
to avoid a certain sympathy with it.[1] As it took place, hundreds of
intellectuals and connoisseurs, artists and poets, architects and
sculptors, musicians and dancers, artisans and craftsmen, crossed
the narrow but perilously seething strait between Java and Bali.
Their movement produced the greatest concentration of talent ever
known in Asia, setting artistic standards which are among the world's
most exacting, and which have never been deviated from. In 1639,
what remained of the royalty and nobility of Majapahit shifted
likewise to Bali, signifying the end of an epoch, the glory of which
was only exceeded by the ruin it caused.

The Hindu–Buddhist period in Java was, in fact, in the Austronesian context, a magnificent excrescence; and the refugees in
Bali were sharply reminded of it. There they returned to the ancestral traditions, in which, while demons and monstrosities are sculpted, the gods are not. As the *chandi bentár*, Bali's distinctive split
gate, denotes, what is of importance in the intangible world is
invisible, beyond the reach of even the most skilled human hand.

Islam's replacement of what it destroyed being culturally negligible, Java never recovered from the revolution that ended the Hindu
epoch. From that day to this, the society, arts and culture of Java
have remained an imperfect reflexion of what achieves fulfilment in
Bali, the consummate masterpiece of the Austronesian world in
Asia, one of the most perfectly balanced and gifted societies on
earth.

Nor did the Muslim revolution bring any such benefits as may
have been expected. Despite caste being abolished wherever a community became Muslim, the two castes in effect remained, as they
do to this day. Marriage between the two is negligible, no longer for

[1] Islam's successful spread in South-East Asia has to be seen against the prevailing esoteric Hindu–Buddhist ambience, which ignored nine-tenths of the population, and had gone to seed in an undergrowth of dreams, portents, and mysticism.
By contrast, Islam presented a religion compelling in its modernity, factualness,
absence of superstitition, and above all, application to everybody. On South-East
Asia at that time it had rather the same effect as Darwin. It did away with myth.

religious reasons, but because these are two pronouncedly different social classes, between whom there is no real marital compatibility in terms of society.

Among the Bugis of Celebes the two castes re-formalized themselves under Islam in the division between royal and commoner families. The number of times Bugis princesses are encountered in history conveys the impression of a royal family of inexhaustible fertility. In fact, the appellation merely denotes a lady of the former upper caste, which was on marrying terms with royalty.

The unequal numerical balance of these social divisions would everywhere have lessened with time, as they widely have among tribal people, had it not been for the Austronesian arrival in Asia. This had the accidental effect of giving extreme caste divisions an extended lease of life.

The result is that, wherever people with a Pacific background are to be found in Asia – markedly in Indonesia, the Philippines, and Malaysia, evident in Cambodia, and distantly evident even in Japan – society consists of the toiling millions at ground level with, suspended far above them in a balloon, a small group of leaders and organizers. The balloon is moored to the earth by a cable, indicating that the two groups belong to the same nation, a fact which might otherwise be open to doubt.

By a curious twist of history, in the two places where caste is recognized for what it is – Ceylon and Bali – society is balanced, everyone at ground level. The irony of it is that the situation is not, in origin, Oceanic.

18 Return to the Pacific

It remains to relate what happened to the people whose traditions and life have been used here to explain the nature of Austronesia, and the link between the Pacific and Southern Asia – the people of the Gilbert Islands.

The ancestors of the Gilbertese were part of a large group from Samoa, who during the Austronesian period settled in the Moluccas. Their most favoured home there, which their traditions describe as a paradisal island, was Buru, of which they seem to have been the principal inhabitants. They were also settled on Amboina and Ceram (Serang) immediately to the east, on Halmahera to the north, and on Vaihiu (Waigeo), situated off the north-western tip of New Guinea. These latter islands they shared with Melanesians, with whom they did not intermarry. They did, however, intermarry with Asians.

Exceptionally conservative in temperament, less involved in Asiatic affairs than were those who had settled further west, they remembered their Samoan origin, their religious ideas, and their clans; and they preserved, over a period of many centuries, a faint knowledge of how to return to Samoa.

This could be done by sailing due north from Vaihiu toward such remote dots as the Palau Islands and Yap, until encountering the eastward current, which would bear them through remote and lonely Micronesia as far as the Marshall Islands, where a southward course could be taken to the Gilberts, thence south-eastward another 1,300 miles to Samoa, a total journey of more than 5,000 miles.

Around 450 B.C., evidently disillusioned by the changed conditions brought about by the steadily expanding activities of the continental civilizations, for which they saw they were no match, with their trade crippled, and doubtless for other reasons which are no longer apparent, a movement arose among them to make a desperate attempt to return to ancestral Samoa.

It was a movement which probably took about a century to effect, and caused great disorder throughout Micronesia, as one group of evacuees after another, despairing of the difficulties of reaching Samoa, took the easy way out by invading and conquering lone islands and atolls, only to be thrown out in due course by others bent on reaching the same destination.

In disorder and strife they penetrated eastward, establishing themselves wherever they could, giving Micronesia the characteristic it bears to this day of being inhabited by people about whom there is something faintly Indonesian – a 'mixed race' character which distinguishes them from others in the Pacific.

A large group reached and conquered the Gilberts, throwing out many of the inhabitants, some of whose ideas became absorbed into their own. But they were still too numerous for the land available. In the Gilberts they divided, one group remaining, the other carrying on till they reached Samoa.

There they managed to ensconce themselves on the principal islands of Savai'i and Upolu, alongside the existing inhabitants.

These, however, their ancestral relatives, had changed profoundly over the centuries. To start with, they looked different, due to inter-marriage with others who had entered the Pacific from South America after the Austronesian period. These gave Polynesia its character, then as now, of which an important feature is group sense.

All important activity among the Samoans was performed, on an instinctive basis, in groups, something entirely foreign to the returnees, and to which they did not adapt.

Religious ideas, while still ancestral, had changed markedly. With these changes, too, the returnees did not agree. Furthermore, a cannibal cult had come into existence in Samoa. As this developed, it became increasingly a point of difference between resident and returnee. The Austronesian civilization had had no connexion with perverse cults of this kind.

The returnees were not simply conservative. For centuries in Asia they had preserved elements of their ancient culture and traditions, with the intensity which ever accompanies conservatism in foreign surroundings. They returned to Samoa to find themselves in the position of the displaced person who, coming home, finds that he has proudly maintained in foreign parts traditions and manners which at home no longer matter.

The experience strengthened their conservatism, providing one of the reasons why their traditions have come down through such an immensity of time.

This uneasy situation of two related yet unrelated communities prevailed in Samoa for a remarkably long period, worsening as the cannibal cult took more hold. Finally, around A.D. 850, after several decades of internal disorder, there was an uprising, in which the returnee descendants were thrown out.

They evidently put up a stiff fight, being able to evacuate a certain number of their women and children. But they were pursued at sea with such vigour that they scattered, never to re-group. The less experienced drifted in many directions, one group ending up in New Zealand. The community's leaders, with more experience, made for their 'mixed race' brethren, the nearest of whom were in the Gilbert Islands.

There followed the most decisive invasion and conquest in Gilbertese prehistory, in which the invaders from Samoa vanquished those who resisted them, making themselves masters of the atolls.

Around 1550 there was a further invasion, this time internal. A group from Béru, in the Southern Gilberts, conquered every atoll as far north as Tárawa. The genealogies of nearly everyone in the Central Gilberts today date in detail to the Béru conquest.[1]

From the 1830s onwards, with the coming of European traders, beachcombers and slavers, bringing firearms and intoxicating liquor, a number of the atolls sank into a state of complete internal disorder, until 1892, when a British protectorate was declared over them. They remain to this day a British possession. In 1943, Tárawa, the principal atoll, was the scene of one of the most destructive and terrible battles of the Pacific War.

Their population at the last census (1967) was 55,000, and it was rising at the alarming rate of 3% per year, indicating a return to the

[1] See Appendix 5: Pacific Genealogies.

Pacific's eternal problem of over-population, which was where this story began.

The Gilbert Islands were named after Captain Thomas Gilbert, commander of one of two East India Company ships which, in 1788, having offloaded the first convicts in Australia, passed through the atolls on their way to China to load tea for the British market.

Their real name is Tungáru. Indicative of the millennia of mystery to which they provide a door, the name Tungáru is so old that no one knows what it means.

APPENDIX

I

Perverse Cults

Cannibalism, head-hunting, human sacrifice and the like do not relate to man in the earliest stage of his formed societies. They are later-introduced cults, resulting in every instance from wilful perversions of established ideas.

Head-collecting was simply an illiterate society's method of assembling war trophies, the heads of fallen enemies being the equivalent of captured standards in European wars. Head-hunting, on the other hand, is a perverse cult. There is no detectable sign of it, either in Borneo or the Solomon Islands, prior to the 15th century A.D., and in both places its origin was the same. It was a perversion of the idea of *mana*.

Mana is unitary and qualitative. A grain of rice contains *mana*. By holding a grain of rice in the palm of one's hand, and adding more grains to it, nothing has been done to increase the *mana* in a grain of rice.

The most powerful repository of *mana* is the human head. The skulls of enemies who died valiantly were strong in *mana*, and a skullhouse containing many of these was specially strong. From this the perverted mind of some unknown divinator, perhaps a member of a tribe which was not faring well, conceived the idea that to amass more skulls would increase the tribe's *mana*, leading to the indiscriminate amassing of human heads, from outside the tribe. As all ideas do, particularly degenerate ones, it quickly spread, reducing wide areas to a state of desperate insecurity, lowering the entire quality of human life, as well as giving rise to absurd practices such as the refusal of any girl to accept a man's advances unless he presented her with a human head, be it only that of an old woman whom he had hit from behind while she was drawing water from a stream.

The perversion of thought here was that *mana*, which is unitary and qualitative, was distorted into the quantitative and accumulatory, entirely depriving it of meaning.

The two principal authorities on the Gilbert Islands – Père Ernest Sabatier, of the French Marist Mission, and Sir Arthur Grimble – held divergent views on cannibalism. Grimble considered there was evidence of a previous cannibal cult in the atolls, while Sabatier, who lived the greater part of his life in the Gilberts and was particularly interested in this point, could find no trace of it. Isolated instances of cannibalism there were in the past. In each case the malefactor was punished, either by being killed or thrown off the atoll, one man taking the law into his own hands for the good of all; and Sabatier noted that the names of such men were invariably remembered with thankfulness and respect. His conclusion was that the Gilbertese had always regarded cannibalism with abhorrence.

A difficulty in the Gilberts is that memory stretches back so far that it is often difficult to tell whether a memory relates to something that happened in the atolls, or in Samoa, or even in Buru. The Grimble evidence, in my opinion, refers to Samoa, where there was definitely a cannibal cult; see Part IV, Chap. 11.

The cannibal cults which Bougainville and Cook discovered in the Pacific were symptomatic of cultures which, due to long isolation, had sunk into a state of morbid decay. The Austronesian languages of today speak for themselves. No culture could have made so deep an impact over so vast a region if it had been a purveyor of morbidity.

2

Melanesian Thought

In accord with the use of the word 'man' in sole relation to one's own tribe, every Melanesian tribal group had its own account of man's arrival on earth, and each account is intensely local. The first man (implying the first woman as well) came from between two tall trees which used to rise on *that* hill, someone will explain, and will point to the hill. Twenty miles further on, from another tribe, may come the assertion that the first man came out of a giant clamshell which once lay on the beach on that promontory over *there*, and the informant will similarly point to it. Many of the tribal names to this day are simply archaic words meaning 'man'.

Melanesian creation stories contain nothing supernatural. In the sense that there is no Creator, they are not really creation stories. Man simply *is*. He does not arrive from anywhere. There is a moment in past time when he *is*. This is preceded by a time when he is *not*. In Malinowski's Trobriand Islands man came out of holes in the earth. Nowhere did he come by boat, or from anywhere else.

In matriarchal societies – as in the Trobriands – where the first man and woman were often brother and sister, the first woman was impregnated either by water dripping from a stalactite, or by the rays of the sun, or by some equally unusual but 'scientifically' explained method, entirely devoid of the supernatural in the deistic sense.

There was a sense that the sky, being above, was superior; and the suggestion that man in after-life mounted into the sky. The hawk enjoyed a special esteem among birds on this account, because it flew highest. In some places there was an invisible island to which the dead went, and whence in due course they returned to live again, entering the mother through the head, then lodging in the womb. But thought as 'advanced' as this was somewhat unusual.

Equally 'scientific' was *mana*. Though a spirit, *mana* was strictly related to the natural. It was a scientific explanation of the intangible factor in life, based exclusively on visible and tactile evidence. In some ways Melanesian ideas are surprisingly like our own today. They seldom presumed into what could not be demonstrated.

Tambu (*tabu*, or taboo) was similarly 'scientific'. It rested in the certain knowledge that restraint or temporary abstinence from certain activities strengthens the performance of them.

In all of this one sees the human mind, in thousands of small tribal sections, at work on the visible and tactile data with which man, originally a pioneer being, a new animal, found himself confronted.

3
Language and War in Melanesia

The date of the Melanesian Reaction, marking the start of Melanesia's long period of isolation from others, is immediately related to the fissiparation of language which resulted from that isolation, coupled with the fact that Melanesia, after the period of Austronesian peace, sank into conditions of near-total hostility.

There are islands in the New Hebrides where people live on the tops of spines descending from hill ranges, each group having its own language variant, one group being within shouting distance of the next. Group A, on top of one spine, will understand Group B on top of the next, and these will understand Group C on the next. But for a man of Group A to speak to someone from Group C, difficulties are already starting; and by the time one reaches Group G at the other end of the island, the language is incomprehensible to Group A, scarcely less so to Group B. The distance between Groups A and G may well be less than 20 miles.

These seven dialects, plus another five on the spines descending from the same central hill range on the other side of the island, are variants of a single Austronesian-derived language once spoken by everyone on the island.

During the period of isolation, the only peaceful intercourse such people had was through marriage, which was exogamous, though confined to direct neighbours. This is to say, there would be marriage ties between Groups A and B, and between B and C, but none between A and C.

The only other intercourse they had was war, usually concerned with tribal boundaries. War in Melanesia was a formal affair, unlike war anywhere else. A challenge would be issued in the drum code, a place and date fixed in advance for the encounter, and preparations made. These included ensuring on both sides that women and small children were kept well out of the danger zone, the sanctity of women and small children being recognized by all. Fighting was often concerned with a boundary line which the challengers contested, and which the defenders would sometimes mark by sticking spears or stakes along it. The idea of annihilation ran counter to ideas of war, as did total occupation of enemy territory. Though penetration of enemy territory in the course of a battle might be relatively deep, the affray ended with mutual withdrawal to home ground, the boundaries of which might, as a result of the battle, be temporarily altered.

Combinations of tribes to fight others were rare, and such combinations did not last. Tribes seldom fused in friendship, and no tribe extended its sway by dominating the lives and possessions of others. Though tribes fought, in a curious way things remained as they were.

In these strange circumstances, language as spoken on each spine descending from the hill range developed in its own separateness. Language spoken by Group A at one end of the island slowly changed from the original in its own way, while among Group G at the other end of the island language was changing in a slightly different way, the same occurring on each spine, a process on which the only outside influence was from immediate neighbours who were within shouting distance. Slowly the original tongue span out till Groups A and G, the furthest apart, reached the mutually incomprehensible.

The question is: how long did it take for this to happen?

In the 1940s the eminent philologist and Anglican missionary Dr. Charles E. Fox compiled a dictionary of the Arosi language, spoken in part of San Cristóbal in the Solomon Islands. Exactly a hundred years previously, the French missionary Verguet, a member of the first and ill-fated French Catholic mission to the Solomons – most of the missionaries were killed, and some were eaten – had made a dictionary of the same language, enabling comparison to be made in ideal conditions. In the century which had elapsed between the two dictionaries, only one word in the Arosi language had changed, and this word only by one letter.

This is an incredibly slow rate of change, the outcome of profound cultural isolation. These are languages which have literally stewed in their own juice for centuries.

The Arosi language is spoken over a wider area than are the New Hebrides spinal dialects, but the conditions of cultural isolation are not dissimilar. In the Solomons, though warriors were often seaborne, war had the same feature that total occupation of enemy territory was a concept unknown. There are reasonable grounds for supposing that this rate of change of one word per century is representative of much of the region.

Applying it therefore to the spinal dialects in the New Hebrides, where it can be seen for certain that all the dialects are descended from the same branch of the same parent tongue, and considering that Groups A and G were the first to reach mutual incomprehension, it might be assumed that this point would have been reached when 50% of all the words in the original language had changed. Allowing that change, along slightly different lines, was taking place in both dialects, this would mean that the incomprehension point would be reached when 25% of the words in each dialect had altered – different words, producing a total of 50% between the two.

For 25% of the words in a language of 1,700 words to change at a rate of one word per century would take 4,200 years. This is assuming that *different* words were changing in Groups A and G, a mechanistic approach which is somewhat unlikely in reality. The change could have taken much longer than this. In addition, there is the difficulty with Austronesian languages that, due to their affixes and suffixes, the number of actual words in a language is a matter of interpretation. The number 1,700 is small – Dr. Fox's Arosi dictionary contains 25,000 words – being based on an assessment of words in common use.

Confining consideration to the shortest time possibility, and allowing that fissiparation did not start immediately after isolation, to allow 5,000 years for the point of incomprehension to be reached is not unreasonable. It errs on the side of caution.

It is for these reasons that, both here and in an earlier work, *Western Pacific Islands*, I have given the approximate date 3000 B.C. as marking the commencement of the fissiparation of language in Melanesia, which of itself marks the beginning of the period of isolation.

4

Hinduism in Indonesia

Up to the present time, historians have not been able to place Hindu influence in Indonesia earlier than the first century A.D. Tradition is emphatic that irrigation and the domesticated buffalo were introduced from India, and recent research has shown that irrigation in Java is several centuries older than the first century A.D.

The date 800 B.C. given here for the introduction of irrigation is based on the probable age of the oldest irrigation works, combined with an assessment of how long it would have taken for Old Hinduism to have established itself, and for Java to have become a Hindu island. The nature of Old Hinduism is based on an examination of conditions in Flores.

The association between the reign of Ashoka and the arrival of Brahmins in Java is an inevitable one. There is nothing known in Indian history in the first century A.D. which could have prompted such a move.

It receives confirmation in the words of an ancient song in the language of Sika, spoken in a part of eastern Flores. This song, which is of great historical interest and importance, tells the story of the arrival of the Sika people, or a section of them.

Here is a condensed version of it:

> We are people of Bangla, who dwelt where the islands meet the sea. We fled from our homes in face of the invasion of the white men from the North. It was a time of great carnage; the earth stank with rotting corpses. In our boats, bearing our women and children with us, we journeyed southward in great hardship, till we reached Bura, where we found conditions were the same, and we were again forced to flee. We withdrew to the land of iron, where we stayed for some time, till we came to this land, where we were welcomed and made a home.

Bangla is Bengal. 'Where the islands meet the sea' is the Sundarbans, which at their southern extremities are very much like islands. The 'white men from the North' are the White Huns, whose invasion of Bengal, hitherto uncertain in history, would have taken place in the second century B.C.

Bura is Java, or a part of it. Prior to the coming of Europeans, none of the larger islands had names. Geographical identification was based on people and the language they spoke. Bura was a part of Java in which a language called Bura was spoken.

'Where we found conditions were the same' does not refer to invasion by the White Huns, who did not invade Indonesia. By the veiled and discreet way in which this phrase occurs, it discloses that the group concerned were of a low caste subject to persecution. Though the invasion of the White Huns was the immediate cause of their flight, they were already in a position of misfortune. In Java they found they were in the same position, subject to persecution, whereas in Flores, under Old Hinduism, they were not.

This is a plain indication that Java in the second century B.C. was already under Brahminical Hinduism. Brahmins, with their high ideas of purity, have ever been the most extreme in relation to persecuted castes. As evidenced by conditions in Bali, when the Dutch assumed administration there in 1908, caste law was severe, inter-caste sexual contact being punishable by death. There is every reason to suppose that the same was true of Java under Brahminical Hinduism.

The 'land of iron', to which they withdrew, is Kedáh, on the west coast of the Malay peninsula. Known today for its tin, in former times Kedáh was famed for iron, which was being worked in pre-Roman times.

The fact that the refugees had to withdraw so far from Java indicates how widespread Brahminical Hinduism was. It was not possible for them to pass from Bura to another part of Java, or even to southern Sumatra. Only in Kedáh were they free of Brahmin influence, and there only to some extent, as their subsequent move to Flores suggests. There, in conditions of Old Hinduism, free of Brahmins, they found a welcome and a home.

I am grateful to Oscar Pareira Mandalangi, of Maumeré, Flores, for drawing my attention to this song. He, his father, and his grandfather have over the years made it their spare-time occupation to collect the ancient Sika songs, and record the words of them in writing. Hitherto unpublished, the collection is of exceptional interest, deserving of more attention than it has received.

5

Pacific Genealogies

The dates given for the various prehistoric movements of the Gilbertese are based on their genealogies. These dates differ from those suggested by Sir Arthur Grimble, and as given in official publications and other works on the subject, in that an enlarged generation period has been used.

Among those using Pacific genealogies as a means of establishing approximate dates in the prehistoric past, it has been the practice to use a 25-year generation period.

In 1954–5 I did a survey of 250 South Chinese villages, in what was then the Southern District of the New Territories of Hongkong, with a view to establishing their foundation dates, and to building up a better knowledge of the history of the region. There was the advantage that dates arrived at by generations could in many cases be checked against known events in history. The survey revealed with complete consistency across the entire district a generation period of 33. When at the end I questioned the senior elders of the district on the matter, they expressed surprise that I did not know that 33 years was a generation period.

The generation length here is largely accounted for by infant mortality, as well as to a lesser extent by pestilence and occasional natural disasters. It has to be seen, however, against conditions of very early marriage, eighteen being a normal age during the Ming and Ch'ing dynasties for a Chinese woman to bear her first child.

On Pacific atolls as difficult as the Gilberts, there was a similar degree of infant mortality. In addition, the rate of loss at sea was surprisingly high, so much so that in the 1920s the British authorities in the Gilberts felt obliged to prohibit small-craft journeys from atoll to atoll within the group. People married young; but as the Chinese instance shows, this of itself is not necessarily an influencing factor amid such general conditions.

In addition, an important Pacific clan genealogy does not descend in the line of eldest sons. It descends in the line of men who achieved something notable; and such could be seventh or eighth sons, and often were.

All told, there is a parallel with Chinese conditions, and for this reason I am of the opinion that, in reading prehistoric dates into Pacific genealogies, a period longer than 25 years is required to denote a generation.

When I came to write about the prehistory and history of the Gilbert Islands,[1] I decided to apply to the Gilbertese genealogies the 33-year Chinese generation period. This gave approximately 450 B.C. as the date of the departure from the Moluccas, and made immediate historical sense in relation to events in Asia, which the earlier-given date, based on a 25-year generation period, did not.

What the real generation period is – or was, before European times – in any part of the Pacific will never be known for certain; but somewhere between 30 and 33 years seems the most likely.

[1] In *Western Pacific Islands*. This work was jointly commissioned by Her Majesty's Government and the Western Pacific administrations.

6

Early Trade with Insular Asia

Prefacing Part III, I have placed a quotation from John Masefield's *Cargoes*. The period referred to is rather 'late' in prehistory, but the verse gives a vivid and accurate impression of what was taking place in Insular Asia at the time.

The triremes and quinquiremes of Nineveh and other places roved more widely than has hitherto been appreciated. Ophir is almost certainly the Malay peninsula. The Portuguese, as a result of detailed inquiries carried out after their occupation of Malacca in 1511, were convinced of this. They named the prominent mountain in the hinterland Mount Ophir, a name it bears to this day, and they were particularly impressed by the remains of worked-out gold mines which they found at the foot of this mountain. Wild peacocks, incidentally, are still to be found in this locality.

Points on this west coast of Malaya were used for the collection of gold, and as staging points on the journey to and from Timor, whence sandalwood.

All major trade voyages in early times were made in rowed vessels, continental Asians having originally followed the example of the Austronesians, whose vessels and methods they then ingeniously elaborated on. Note too – apes and peacocks – the frivolous aspect of early trade.

Whether triremes, etc., reached China is doubtful. Continental Asians were not such expert sailors as Austronesians, nor were they prepared to rough it in open boats, like the latter. They probably hesitated to risk the uncertainties of the South China Sea.

They certainly made it to Timor, however. At Dobo, a hill village in the Maumeré district of Flores, is preserved a finely-wrought bronze model of a Nineveh trireme of great age, complete with bronze captain and officers, wearing their distinctive uniform, and rowers. Either it was carried for luck, or – perhaps more probably – it was the toy of a wealthy child. It was found several hundred years ago on the beach off Endé, on the south side of Flores, directly on the route to Timor. Presumably the parent vessel suffered a disaster.

I am indebted to the Indonesian authorities of Flores for enabling me to see this valuable and wonderful relic which, due to its powerful magic qualities – to which Dobo attributes its prosperity – is kept permanently hidden in a forest, from which only one man knows how to fetch it.

7

Agastya

On the following page will be found a line drawing of a statue of Agastya, from the Chandi Banon in South Kedu, Java.

Agastya was the Indian who did more than anyone else to establish and promote Brahminical Hinduism in Java. After his death he was venerated there under the apellation Bhatara Guru, or Siva Guru. Bhatara, or Batara, both in Indonesia and the Philippines, is a name given to supreme deity. Its application to Agastya places him, in the Hindu context, as an aspect of supreme deity, superior even to the Hindu Trinity. While little is known of the details of his life, it is clear that he must have been a person of immense influence.

In the statue, made many centuries after his death, the sculptor was obliged to follow with the greatest exactitude every detail handed down by tradition concerning Agastya, exactly as European artists did with Christ, due to the veneration accorded him. The result is a remarkable and lifelike posthumous portrait of the most memorable figure in Further India.

It is axiomatic in Hindu thought to judge by initial impressions, which to the Twice-Born are the surest. Moreover, it would have been unseemly to have conveyed Agastya as the frail old man he doubtless became. This is clearly a statue of Agastya as he was when he first arrived from India.

He is middle-aged, a tall, well-built, broad-shouldered, imposing man, becoming rather portly. The high bridge of his nose indicates a Northern Indian. He is bearded, but shaves with particular care round the mouth, so as to eat with perfect cleanliness.

He is naked to the waist, as was the Brahmin custom in hot weather; and the way his cloth is tied, with the pleat behind him, again indicates the North. He wears an elaborate, jewel-studded belt, signifying a holder of office at court, of the minimum rank of adviser.

He is a man of wealth. His cloth is bordered with gold thread, and his accoutrements (belt, armlets, ear-rings) are all costly. He wears heavy ear-rings of solid worked silver, the metal of spiritual

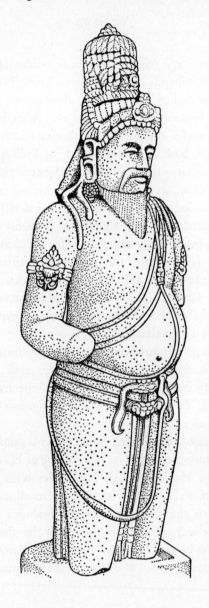

purity; and the weight of these has depressed the lobes of his ears. These lobes have previously broken twice under the weight of such ornaments, the former lobes hanging useless beside the present one, indicating that he has worn such ear-rings from a very early age. This is certainly a person born in circumstances of wealth and high position.

He is a Brahmin, and the way he wears his thread, with the third loop falling well below the other two, indicates that he is from one of the groups who are Brahmins of the Brahmins, i.e. teachers of teachers, the highest rank of the highest caste. The three threads hanging thus indicate that he is master of three of the Vedic disciplines, itself a considerable intellectual accomplishment.

He wears his hair gathered upwards, held in position by a thick ring of worked silver, with a frontal headpiece resembling a coronet. The sculptor has made a subtle play on these elaborate head ornaments to convey a likeness to Brahma, the Originator, in allusion to Agastya's position as the *fons et origo* of orthodox Hinduism in Java. Brahma's other three heads are left out, however, a factor which the sculptor uses to stress without words that this is as near as possible a portrait of an actual man.

Finally, the stance and general presentation of the statue show that Agastya was a Saivite.

The combination of the foregoing details, scrupulously presented by the sculptor, makes it transparently plain that Agastya arrived in Java as a man of eminence in his own country. Everything about the statue indicates authority at the highest level, making it possible in conclusion to say that the ceremonial belt signifies not merely an adviser, but a senior minister. It must be remembered too (see footnote on Prambánan, p. 165) that Hindu sculpture in Java was portraiture, to a degree unknown in India. Thus the historical significance of even the smallest detail.

For these and the other reasons cited in the text of this work, I am of the opinion that Agastya was a senior minister at the court of Ashoka, that he provoked the ire of the Emperor by his resistance to Buddhism, and that he fled the court, finally taking refuge in the Sundarbans, which no Indian military force could penetrate.

To judge by the Javanese statue, he was about fifty by this time. His sons would be grown up, able to take care of their mother. As a Brahmin family man he had fulfilled his duties. Irked by his enforced inactivity, and learning that Java was a Hindu island in need of persons such as he, he sailed forth to become the greatest of all Hindu missionaries and educators overseas.

At the village of Majilpur (or Mozilpur) in the southern part of the 24-Parganas of Bengal, not far from the Sundarbans, the potter includes in his repertoire a statuette of Agastya, exact in every detail, so far as clay will allow.

The art of the Bengal potters is hereditary, following unbroken traditions of several thousand years. One could search the whole of Upper India without finding another such statuette, or indeed any trace of Agastya. The Majilpur statuette is extraordinary, and there must be a historical reason for its existence.

I first visited Majilpur in 1944, and in my first book, *Invitation to an Eastern Feast*, I referred to the statuette, saying its presence there was inexplicable. I have since come to the conclusion that it must indicate direct contact with Agastya himself, in the manner described above.

His actual name was probably not Agastya, and he is not to be confused with the *rishi* Agastya of the *Mahabharata*, who 'crossed the Vindhyas', and brought orthodox Hinduism to South India. It is possible that the name Agastya attached itself to him because he did the same for Java as the *rishi* Agastya is reputed to have done for South India.

Bibliography

The study of the prehistoric cultural contact between the Pacific and Asia demands knowledge and direct experience of five regions: Oceania, Melanesia, South-East Asia, India and China. The following is a selected list of books which may serve as a general introduction to the subject.

First, in a class on their own, come five classic works of original observation and inquiry, given here in the order in which they were written:

TOMÉ PIRES: *Suma Oriental*. Written 1512–15. First published 1944, in English translated from Portuguese by Armando Cortesão, from the only known manuscript in the library of the Chambre des Députés, Paris. 2 vols. Hakluyt Society, London.

ANTONIO DE MORGA: *Sucesos de las Islas Filipinas*. Written 1595–1600. Published in Mexico City, 1609. Recent new translation from Spanish by J. S. Cummins, Hakluyt Society, Cambridge, 1971. Second Series, No. 140.

Captain JAMES COOK: *The Journals of, on his Voyages of Discovery* (1768–80). Edited by J. C. Beaglehole. 4 vols. Hakluyt Society Extra Series, Cambridge.

WILLIAM MARSDEN, F.R.S.: *The History of Sumatra*; London, 1783. The third edition, enlarged and definitive (Longman, London, 1811), has recently been reprinted by Oxford University Press in their Oxford in Asia Historical Reprints series.

Sir THOMAS STAMFORD RAFFLES, F.R.S. and A.S.: *The History of Java*, 2 vols.; East India Company booksellers and John Murray, London, 1817. Reprinted by Oxford, ditto.

On Melanesia:

R. H. CODRINGTON: *The Melanesians*; Oxford, 1891.

Dr. CHARLES E. FOX: *The Threshold of the Pacific*; Kegan Paul, London, 1924. *Kakamora*; Hodder and Stoughton, 1962. The foremost Melanesian philologist of this century, Dr. Fox's main work is to be found in learned journals, the Polynesian Society, etc.

JEAN GUIART: *Un siècle et demie de contacts culturels à Tanna, Nouvelles-Hébrides*; Musée de l'Homme, Paris, 1956.

TOM HARRISSON: *Savage Civilisation*; Gollancz, London, 1937. In particular the chapter entitled 'People', in which the author uses English as far as possible to express Melanesian thoughts.

BRONISLAW MALINOWSKI: *Argonauts of the Western Pacific*; Kegan Paul, 1922. The foundation work on Melanesian ceremonial trade. *Sex and Repression in Savage Society*; ditto, 1927.

W. H. R. RIVERS: *The History of Melanesian Society*; Cambridge, 1914.

On the Gilbert Islands:

Sir ARTHUR GRIMBLE: *A Pattern of Islands*; John Murray, London, 1952.

ROSEMARY GRIMBLE: *Migrations, Myth and Magic from the Gilbert Islands*; early writings of Sir Arthur Grimble, arranged and illustrated; Routledge and Kegan Paul, London, 1972. A reference work of major importance, containing the description of the prehistoric astronomy and navigation course which gives the ancient Pacific its credibility.

ERNEST SABATIER: *Sous l'équateur du Pacifique*; Editions Dillen, Paris, 1939. A history of the Catholic mission in the Gilberts, its particular value, aside from this, lies in the early and more general chapters.

General List:

H. OTLEY BEYER: *Philippine and East Asian Archaeology, and its relation to the origin of the Pacific Islands population*; reprinted National Research Council, Philippines, Dec. 1948, Bulletin 29. The foremost ethnographer of the Philippines, the major part of Beyer's work was unpublished at the time of his death. This, together with his collected published work and library, has recently been purchased by the National Library of Australia.

C. A. BAMPFYLDE and S. BARING-GOULD: *Sarawak and its Two White Rajahs*; London, 1909.

Sir ROBERT BLACKWOOD: *Beautiful Bali*; Cassell, Melbourne, 1970. Written to serve as a guidebook, it contains succinct and accurate explanations of Balinese religion and society.

Sir JOHN BOWRING, F.R.S.: *The Kingdom and People of Siam*, 2 vols.; London, 1856. Re-issued, Oxford in Asia Historical Reprints.

AUSTIN COATES: *Invitation to an Eastern Feast*; Hutchinson, London, 1953; Harper, New York, 1954. In particular, Part Three on Hinduism. *Western Pacific Islands*; H.M. Stationery Office, London (Corona Library series), 1970. On Melanesian thought, Chaps. 10 and 11.

G. COEDÈS: *Les états hindouisés d'Indochine et d'Indonésie*; Paris, 1948. *Les peuples de la péninsule indochinoise*; Paris, 1962. The master historian who has done more than anyone to unravel South-East Asia's past.

ONOFRE D. CORPUZ: *The Philippines*; Prentice-Hall, New York, 1965.

MIGUEL COVARRUBIAS: *Island of Bali*; Cassell, London, 1937.

C. P. FITZGERALD: *China, A Short Cultural History*; Cresset Press, London, 1935.

O. C. GANGOLY: *The Art of Java*; Rupam, Calcutta, undated, *circa* 1935. The most eminent Indian authority on Hindu art in Indonesia. See also numerous articles of the 1920s, when he was editor of the art magazine *Rupam*.

W. R. GEDDES: *Nine Dayak Nights*; Oxford, 1957. *The Land Dayaks of Sarawak*; H.M. Stationery Office, London.

CLIFFORD GEERTZ: *The Religion of Java*; Free Press, New York, 1960.

D. G. E. HALL: *A History of South-East Asia*; Macmillan, London, 1955.

G. E. HARVEY: *The History of Burma*; Longman, London, 1925.

E. B. HAVELL: *Indian Sculpture and Painting*; John Murray, London, 1908. *The Ideals of Indian Art*; ditto, 1911. These two works, which have never been excelled, are essential to an understanding of Hinduism in relation to art, which in Indonesia is a form of historical literature.

R. VON HEINE-GELDERN: *Prehistoric Research in the Netherlands Indies*; New York, 1945.

THOR HEYERDAHL: *The Kon-Tiki Expedition*; 1948. *American Indians in the Pacific*; 1952.

FEODOR JAGOR: *Reisen in den Philippinen*; Berlin, 1873.

WALTER KAUDERN: *Structures and Settlements in Central Celebes*; Göteborg, 1925.

WILLIAM KNIGHTON: *The History of Ceylon*; Longman, London, 1845.

DELIA and FERDINAND KUHN: *The Philippines*; Holt, Rinehart and Winston, New York, 1966.

J. KUNST: *Music in Flores*; Leiden, 1938. To anyone wishing to go deeply into this region's past, this subject deserves careful scrutiny.

MAHATHIR BIN MOHAMAD: *The Malay Dilemma*; Asia Pacific Press, Singapore, 1970. In particular the chapter on code of ethics and value systems.

ROSALIND MOSS: *The Life after Death in Oceania and the Malay Archipelago*; Oxford, 1925.

C. F. OLDHAM: *The Sun and the Serpent*; Constable, London, 1905.

H. PARKER: *Ancient Ceylon*; Luzac, London, 1909. *Village Folk-Tales of Ceylon*, 3 vols.; ditto, 1910.

W. J. PERRY: *The Megalithic Culture of Indonesia*; Longman, London, 1918.

JEAN POUJADE: *La route des Indes et ses navires*; Payot, Paris, 1946.

Father FERNÃO DE QUEYRÓZ: *Conquista Temporal e Espiritual de Ceylão*, 6 vols.; Government Printer, Colombo, 1916.

NAJEEB M. SALEEBY: *The History of Sulu*; 1908. Reprinted, Filipiniana Book Guild, Manila, 1963.

G. B. SANSOM: *Japan, A Short Cultural History*; Cresset Press, London, 1931.

ANDREW SHARP: *Ancient Voyagers in the Pacific*; Polynesian Society, Wellington, 1956.

W. F. STUTTERHEIM: *Studies in Indonesian Archaeology*; Martinus Nijhoff, The Hague, 1956.

Sir JAMES EMERSON TENNENT: *Ceylon, An Account of the Island, Physical, Historical and Topographical*, 2 vols.; Longman, London, 1860.

ALAN VILLIERS: *The Coral Sea*; Museum Press, London, 1949. Included as a reminder on Pacific studies: if you are not a sailor, read books by people who are.

FRITZ A. WAGNER: *Indonesia, The Art of an Island Group*; Methuen, London, 1959.

H. G. QUARITCH WALES: *The Making of Greater India*; Bernard Quaritch, London, 1951. *Prehistory and Religion in South-East Asia*; ditto, 1957.

Sir RICHARD WINSTEDT: *Shaman Saiva and Sufi*; Constable, London, 1925. *The Malays, A Cultural History*; Singapore, 1947.

SUTJIPTO WIRJOSUPARTO: *Glimpses of Cultural History of Indonesia*; Indira, Jakarta, 1964.

O. W. WOLTERS: *The Fall of Srivijaya in Malay History*; Lund Humphries, London, 1970.

AILSA ZAINU'DDIN: *A Short History of Indonesia*; Cassell, Melbourne, 1968.

Index

Philippine Islands (*cont.*)
127, structure of caste society in 131–134, irrigation in 152–3, and Old Hinduism 156–8, 170

Phoenicians, 136

Pig, 43, 104, and *mana* 117, man's first friend 125–6, 128

Pires, Tomé, first Portuguese envoy to China (1517), 87

Pleiades, 47, 113

Polo, Marco, 167

Polynesia, 31, 103, 104, 105, 107, 120

Portugal, 23, 25, 89, 90, 168

Prambánan, 41, 165 and fn., 190

Prapancha, 161

Rakyat, meaning of 150 fn.

Ramayana, 142, 160 and fn.

Religion (Oceanic), see Ancestors

Rice, 27, 28, 61, 81–2, shifting cultivation of 133–4, 143, 144–6

Rice-measurers, 82, 83, 91

Rizal, José, 100 fn.

Roti, music in 142

Sabatier, Ernest, 176

Samoa, 103, 107, 171–3, 176

Sanskrit, 22–3, 158–9

Semángat, 35, 148–9

Serang, see Ceram

Shakti, in relation to *mana* 148–9

Shin Arahan, 164

Singapore, 24

Singhala, see Ceylon

Slaves, 36, 130–4, 150

Spain, 20, 22, 23, 25, 73, 119, 132, 157–8

Spice Islands, 25

Solomon Islands, 49, 59, 64, 108, 124, 125 fn., 127, 175

South America, Gilbertese expedition to 60–1

Sri Vijaya empire, 84–7, 150

Sudra caste, 146, in Java 161–2

Sukarno, 100 fn.

Sumatra, 10, 61, 63, 64, 65, 77, 79, 84, 99, 100, 120, 122, 126, 127, 145, 146, 152, Buddhism in 163, 168

Sundarbans (forests at mouths of Ganges) 145–6, 155, 191

Tagálog, 120, 159

Tahiti, 3, 60 fn., 103, 106 fn., 107, 110

Taiwan, 9, 69, 71

Tantra, 157 fn., 158

Tao (Philippines), 132, meaning of 150 fn.

Tárawa, 93, 173

Taro, see also *babai*, 33, 34, 104, and *mana* 117, replaced by rice as cereal 133

Tenzing, 52

Ternaté, 89–90

Thailand, 9, 11, 70, 71, 84, 119

Theft, 116–17

Tidor, 89, 90

Time, 26–8, 46–9, 67

Timor, 10, 80, 104, 142, 147 fn., caste names in 149–50, 151, 152, 156, 187–8

Tonga, 103

Tonlé Sap, 61

Torája, 66, 119

Trade, 14, 15, 24, 25, ceremonial 49–54, in Borneo 66, prehistoric development of 68 *et seq.*, effect on Insular Asian society 81 *et seq.*, and on poor diet 88, decline of ceremonial 143

Tuamotu, 105, 107 fn.

Valmiki, 160 fn.

Vedda, 82

Vietnam, 9, 11, 70, 71, 119

War, 64, in atolls 107, in Melanesia 116, 118, 179–80

White Huns, 155, 183

Yung Lo, Ming Emperor of China (1402–24), 167